Rails to the Forest

Railways of the Forest of Dean

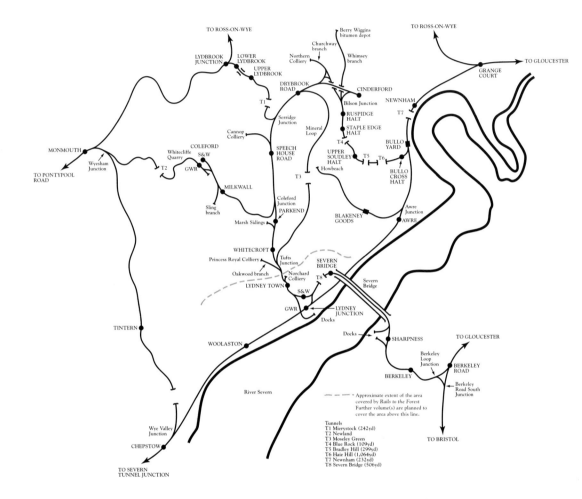

Rails to the Forest

The Severn & Wye Railway from Berkeley Road to Norchard 1945-2010

Dean Forest Railway Museum Trust

Silver Link Publishing Ltd

First published in 2010

British Library Cataloguing in Publication Data
A catalogue record for this book is available from the British Library.

ISBN 978 1 85794 345 0

Silver Link Publishing Ltd
The Trundle
Ringstead Road
Great Addington
Kettering
Northants NN14 4BW

Tel/Fax: 01536 330588
email: sales@nostalgiacollection.com
Website: www.nostalgiacollection.com
Printed and bound in the Czech Republic

Acknowledgements

The varied content of the illustrations now featured in this volume has only been possible thanks to the input of many members of the Dean Forest Railway Society, both past and present. All images have been duly credited wherever possible, but if there are any errors or omissions, do please advise. Valued assistance and co-operation has also been readily forthcoming from the Dean Heritage Museum, Coleford Railway Museum, and Gloucester County Archives. Thanks are also extended to the Kidderminster Railway Museum, The Industrial Railway Society, The Stephenson Locomotive Society, and Wild Swan Publications for permission to reproduce some of the historic images held in their respective collections. Even enquiries to several former colleagues from schooldays have prompted several more gems to resurface after 45 years or more in the attic. Among those who have provided valued behind-the-scenes assistance have been Ben Ashworth, Stewart Blencowe, David Ponter, Mike Rees, Brian Ward-Ellison and Dr Graham Field, while our principal guru and guide on matters IT has been John Freer. Last, but not least, we must record our sincere thanks and appreciation to artist Rob Rowland for creating the memorable image which now adorns the front cover of this book.

Of equal value to the photographs themselves have been the descriptions of both daily routine railway operations and one-off incidents and events so readily and graphically imparted by former employees from both sides of the Severn. On the S&W lines, as elsewhere, much of their work was carried out strictly in accordance with the Rule Book, but common sense and expediency also played a big part. What is striking now is how so many railwaymen, even long into retirement, still look back upon their careers not as just a job, but as a whole way of life, in which they became members of an extended family with which they still maintain contact. Once again, we must place on record the valued contributions made by former BR employees Bob Barnett, Brian Edwards, John Hale, John Harris, Owen Hudson, Derek Markey, Graham Morgan, Derrick Payne, Dave Sherman and the late Reg Webb.

Finally, we are also indebted to several former employees at Sharpness and Lydney Docks, and also Lydney Tinplate Works, for explaining some of the less well-recorded aspects of past operations on these sites. Among them, we must especially thank Charlie Langford (re Sharpness Dock), and Dennis Powell and John Harris (re Lydney Tinplate Works).

Contents

Introduction   7

1   Berkeley Road   9
2   Berkeley Loop   16
3   Berkeley Station   20
4   Sharpness and its docks   22
5   The Severn Railway Bridge   43
6   Severn Bridge station   52
7   Lydney Junction   56
8   Lydney Docks   72
9   Lydney Yard and Shed   81
10 Lydney Tinplate Works   92
11 Lydney Engine Shed Junction to Lydney Town   97
12 Lydney Town station   101
13 Lydney Town to Norchard   108
14 Norchard   114

Bibliography   128
Abbreviations   128
Index of locations   128

From the river bank: The Severn & Wye Railway's three-quarter-mile-long 'white elephant' which spanned the Severn estuary from 1879 until 1960; in the foreground, the steam-powered swingbridge over the Gloucester & Shropshire canal. *DFR Museum Trust Collection*

Here creating a convincing semblance of a daily spectacle once offered by the 7.00am double-headed goods to Coleford, ex-GWR pannier tanks Nos 7754 and 9681 charge past Middle Forge on 28 September 1997. *RHM*

Introduction

The notion of compiling this book first occurred several years ago upon the realisation that 2010 would mark two important anniversaries concerning the Dean Forest Railway, namely 200 years since the incorporation of the Severn & Wye Railway & Canal Co, and 40 years since the formation of the Dean Forest Railway Preservation Society.

Over recent years the Forest's railways have been well documented, prompting doubts as to whether there would still be any demand for yet another publication. From knowledge of collections still held privately and in museum archives, however, it did seem highly probable that there might still be sufficient material of interest to justify at least one modest volume focussing on the more recent years of the Severn & Wye Railway's history since the end of the Second World War. This initial assessment proved to be a well wide of the mark, for in reality an abundance of material has come to light, most of it previously unpublished, charting many aspects of the changing railway scene over the past 65 years. As a result, the initial concept of one volume has, of necessity, already extended to two. Coverage of the S&W system within this volume has therefore been confined to the former 'main line' from Berkeley Road to Norchard, just north of Lydney, together with the branches to the docks at Sharpness and Lydney, and the GWR's Berkeley Loop. Volume 2 will feature the main line northward from Norchard, through Parkend to Cinderford, together with the Mineral Loop and the branches to Coleford and Lydbrook, and all the sidings and tramroads that served the works, quarries and collieries along the way. We trust readers will forgive the above-average exposure given to the section of the S&W line now operated by the Dean Forest Railway – not least because it has already enjoyed a life extension of more than 40 years compared to the rest of the system west of the Severn.

Despite the 250 pages of text and photographs that this and the succeeding volume will provide, we can at best but scratch the surface of the complex history and development of the industries and rail transport systems that once characterised the Forest of Dean. Serving a geographic area of barely 40 square miles, the evolution and survival of the Severn & Wye Railway over the last 200 years has been just about as complicated and colourful as it is possible to be. Readers aspiring to learn more about the railway's history are therefore recommended to refer to some of the many publications now listed in the Bibliography. But do beware, for the subject can become addictive!

Within the first 60 years of the S&WR's operations, traffic was largely confined to the local transportation of timber, coal and iron from the Forest down to Lydney Docks, with but a modest traffic of general merchandise and provisions in the opposite direction. During those years the railway evolved through three distinct phases, each of which overlapped the next. The first was the 3ft 8in-gauge tramroad system, featuring L-profile wrought-iron rails, which operated with horse power from about 1810 until steam power was tried in 1864. Then, in 1868, under pressure from local industrialists, the S&WR belatedly rebuilt 8 miles of its main line from Lydney Docks to Wimberry Slade to Brunel's 7ft ¼in broad gauge, which it operated with its own steam locomotives. By 1872, however, the S&WR main line through Lydney, by then part of the GWR, was already being converted to 4ft 8½in standard gauge, obliging the S&WR to follow suit the same year.

As the Forest coal trade developed in the 1870s, a brief spell of prosperity enabled the S&WR Co to complete its conversion to standard gauge, with new lines to Coleford and Lydbrook Junction, and a loop line to capture traffic from a string of collieries lying to the west of Cinderford. A somewhat sparse and rudimentary passenger service was also introduced at this time, which initially terminated at an arbitrary point in the woods about a mile short of Cinderford. It was during this era that the unbridled optimism of local coal-owners led to the concept of the Severn Bridge Railway, by means of which it was intended to boost shipments of Forest coal from the newly built Sharpness Dock on the eastern bank of the Severn, and to expand into new markets in the South and East of England via the Midland Railway and its connections. Against all the odds, the three-quarter-mile-long bridge was authorised and built at enormous cost, only to be quickly dubbed the 'white elephant' it proved to be, for the anticipated coal traffic never materialised, while the GWR resolutely declined to use it on any regular basis for another 40 years. The S&WR, meanwhile, had amalgamated with the Severn Bridge Railway to become the Severn & Wye & Severn Bridge Railway, only to face financial meltdown and subsequent salvation when the entire system was taken over jointly by the GWR and Midland Railway in 1894.

Yet all was not lost, for even into the post-Second World War era, long after many of the local industries had closed, the route mileage of the Severn & Wye system still totalled some 40 miles, excluding any of the adjoining GWR lines or colliery sidings. Within that mileage, the S&W still managed to portray what was effectively a fascinating microcosm of the country's contemporary railway scene, serving local collieries, quarries and a tinworks, and maintaining connections to two docks and with two of the 'Big Four' railway companies. The whole system was also still linked together by one of the longest iron bridges in the country. Local goods and passenger trains still ran over that bridge on every day except the Sabbath, when, in wintertime, the route took on a wholly more important role, as diverted expresses to Cardiff, Bristol, Portsmouth and Plymouth rumbled their way from one side of the Severn estuary to the other. And on a few select summer days each year, the S&WR restored contact with its roots, when long-closed stations in the Forest were reopened and locals thronged the platforms to join special trains to Paddington or to seaside resorts down the Bristol Channel.

Even into the early post-war years these and many other S&W operations continued to be managed locally from the hub of the system at Lydney, under the guidance of a special S&WJR Operating Appendix drawn up by the LMS & GW railways back in the 1930s. Joint management of the S&WR from 1894 until 1948 had resulted in a rich and quirky mix of built infrastructure and operating practices, which ensured a continuing source of variety and interest, with half of the system maintained by the GWR and half by the LMS. Where else, for example, could one find passenger trains that ran each day without a guard? Or where the coal trains had GWR employees on the footplate, and an LMS guard and shunter in the brake-van? Or where a complete passenger train could be commandeered between booked workings to form an impromptu staff-only funeral train? Almost to the end, the S&W was a railway with an independent spirit.

Then came the 1960s, a decade in which the railway's fortunes spiralled into near oblivion with almost dizzying speed, as the remaining collieries and Lydney's docks faced closure, and the Severn Bridge route was severed. Next came the uncompromising Beeching Report, which quickly resulted in wholesale closures of goods and passenger facilities, followed in turn by the destruction of much of the railway infrastructure, a process that was ruthlessly implemented with unprecedented zeal. As if to compound the impact of change, the steam locomotive, which had dominated the local railway scene for more than 100 years, finally disappeared, while all remaining signal boxes were closed and razed to the ground.

Within less than a decade the entire S&WR system had been reduced to little more than two long featureless sidings, from Berkeley Road to Sharpness Dock, and from Lydney Junction to Parkend Marsh Sidings. It was against this backdrop 40 years ago that a few determined souls took on the challenge of establishing the Dean Forest Railway Preservation Society to save but a token section of this battered but unbowed little railway. We hope that this book will now enable you to join us to enjoy a little time travel into the recent past.

John Metherall, Curator
Bob Marrows, Compiler

1
Berkeley Road

After its restructuring into a joint railway in August 1894, the Severn & Wye system commenced, not within the Forest of Dean, nor even from the banks of the Severn estuary, but rather improbably from the very foot of the Cotswold escarpment, nearly 4 miles east of the river, at Berkeley Road. This rural location, surrounded to this day by open farmland formerly owned by the Berkeley Estate, was the point at which the Midland Railway's 1875 branch to Sharpness left the Bristol & Gloucester main line.

Viewed here from the short approach drive, which was flanked until the early 1950s by a fortnightly livestock market, Berkeley Road was a typical Brunel wayside station, constructed in red brick with stone dressings in Brunel's Italianate style. This is the main building in June 1954, still in its original as-built form. When first opened by the Bristol & Gloucester Railway (B&GR) in 1844, the station was called Dursley & Berkeley, to serve both market towns, the former some 3 miles distant and the latter 2½. In the following year, to the surprise and eternal consternation of the Great Western Railway, the broad gauge B&GR was snapped up by the Midland Railway to form part of its new strategic main-line

route from Derby to Bristol and Bath, thereby penetrating into the very heart of GWR territory. Berkeley Road remained in Midland Railway ownership to the Grouping in 1923, followed by 25 years under the London Midland & Scottish Railway (LMS), and a further 10 years as part of the London Midland Region of BR. Only in 1958 did the Western Region regain control of the route. In recent times the wheel has turned full circle, for most of the still extant B&GR route now forms part of Network Rail's Great Western Division. *Lens of Sutton Association*

This is one of three such running-in boards at the station that continued to refer to the Severn & Wye Railway until repainted by BR in about 1950. *Real Photographs*

The platform elevation of the Brunel-designed station building had decorative cast-iron brackets supporting the timber-framed canopy, which, in this June 1958 view, appears to be in a somewhat parlous condition. Just visible beyond the running-in board is the 'Prince of Wales' hotel, which pre-dated the railway, being strategically located at the junction of what is now the B4066 from Dursley with the A38 from Birmingham to Bristol. *RHM collection*

In this general view of the original B&GR station, looking north on 13 July 1963, a Newcastle to Paignton express is heading through behind ex-LMS 'Black Five' 4-6-0 No 44660. Of note are the running-in board on the left, with 'Lydney' now obscured as a 'change for' destination, and the up-side shelter recently shorn of its canopy, while that on the main building has also been drastically reduced and now features a corrugated steel fascia. To the right, the upper floor of the rather grand station master's house, designed in a matching style, can just be discerned. Beyond the footbridge, the edging of the later MR platform extension has been cut back, leaving just the original B&GR section still useable for up (Birmingham-bound) stopping services. Closure notices, instigated by the Beeching Report, have yet to be posted, but after 140 years of service this station, together with all others between Gloucester and Mangotsfield, will be completely closed to passenger traffic within 18 months. *RHM*

Looking south-west from below the footbridge, also on 13 July 1963, this view shows more graphically the consequences of BR's 'rationalisation' of the original Brunel station canopies. On the up main, ex-LNER 'B1' Class 4-6-0 No 61394 speeds through with an express from Bristol to Sheffield. During the last few years of steam, such Eastern Region interlopers became a familiar sight on this route, especially on summer Saturdays. Almost hidden by the smoke and steam are the original B&GR skewed brick arch bridge and a 'temporary' Warren girder bridge added by Gloucestershire County Council in 1952 to carry the competing A38 Birmingham-Bristol trunk road over the railway at the south end of the station. *RHM*

By contrast, this early post-war view in the opposite direction, towards Gloucester, helps to illustrate the historic development of the station. On the right is the substantial Brunelian goods shed, where two members of Saltley's '2nd XI' are getting in some much-needed practice while their freight train is recessed in the down sidings. On the left is the Midland Railway's 1875 northward extension of the up platform, with another two provided to serve the Sharpness line. In the background, a former MR 3F 0-6-0 and brake-van, returning after an early-morning trip from Gloucester to Sharpness, await a path onto the up main line. *L. E. Copeland/Wild Swan Publications Ltd*

Viewed from a public foot crossing, this is the double-line junction by which the Severn & Wye left the Bristol & Gloucester main line under the control of Berkeley Road's 45-lever Midland Railway signal box, which replaced an earlier structure in 1900. Tottering over the junction on the hot and thundery afternoon of 13 July 1963 is ex-GWR 0-4-2T No 1409, en route from Gloucester to Sharpness to commence operation of the afternoon branch passenger service. *RHM*

Just over 44 years later, on 1 September 2007, the same viewpoint reveals a very different picture. Gone is the double junction, the signal box and the semaphore signals, all swept away when the new Gloucester Panel Box took control of the area in 1968. On the up main a GNER High Speed Train (which normally worked between King's Cross and Aberdeen) screams past the relay room at 100mph with a Saturdays-only Paignton to Newcastle service. And on the left, opposite the now single-line junction, stands Severn & Wye Joint Railway milepost 0 (from which all distances will now be shown in brackets). Our journey into the Forest begins here. *RHM*

Viewed from the north end of the up platform on 3 June 1957, ex-GWR 0-4-2 tank loco No 1430 and two auto-trailers are waiting to form a morning working back to Lydney, while on the down main an ex-LMS Caprotti-valve Class 5 4-6-0 is heading an express passenger service towards Bristol. Note that the vintage lamp housings are devoid of any oil burners since, during high summer, all stopping services called here during daylight hours only. *A. Jarvis*

This is the southward prospect from a similar vantage point just over a year later, showing the full extent of the MR up platform extension, the S&W line diverging to the right, and the MR timber-framed waiting rooms erected in 1875. Ex-LMS 4F 0-6-0 No 44272 is at the head of the 1.10pm SO 'all stations' from Bristol to Gloucester, connecting here with the 2.15pm SO S&W line auto-train to Lydney Town. Blissfully unaware of what fate has in store, the ardent spotter in the foreground will one day become publicity officer for the Dean Forest Railway Preservation Society (DFRPS). *R. E. Toop, C. Maggs collection*

On another summer's morning in 1957, this is the prospective passenger's first glimpse of the Lydney train, on this occasion headed by a locomotive that five years earlier had starred in Ealing Studios' film *The Titfield Thunderbolt* – former GWR 0-4-2 tank No 1401. In the foreground, spanning the main line but not the branch, is the 1883-vintage MR footbridge, replete with some splendid contemporary oil lamps. *RHM collection*

Making connections: a memorable parting image of this country junction captured one summer's evening in August 1947, with the Lydney train patiently waiting in the S&W platform as an up stopping train rolls in from Bristol. The loco crew look on expectantly from the platform while one of their charges has already established himself on the footplate. Vintage auto-fitted GWR pannier tank No 2080 provides the motive power – it appears to have been a popular steed for the passenger diagrams during the early post-war years. Also apparent from this view is the Midland Railway's generous provision of passenger facilities, with at least three fireplaces incorporated into the company's 1875-built waiting rooms to ensure the winter-time comfort of intending travellers. Following closure of the station in January 1965, all buildings were quickly demolished, except for the goods shed, which lasted another 12 years, and the station master's house, which alone has survived into the 21st century. *W. A. Camwell, courtesy Stephenson Locomotive Society*

Forward again to 13 July 1963, and No 1409 is returning to Berkeley Road with its single auto-trailer, forming the 4.15pm from Sharpness. This view westward from the Breadstone Road bridge shows the former S&W up line still in situ, having been retained since 1931 to provide a long refuge siding for up main-line freight trains, but latterly used, as here, for storing surplus wagons. Following withdrawal of the Sharpness passenger service, the siding connection was removed and the junction with the main line singled in May 1965. Also remarkable, given that the photograph was taken on a summer Saturday afternoon, is that there are, at most, only three cars and one pedal-cyclist evident on the entire quarter-mile or more of the adjacent A38 trunk road visible in this view. *RHM*

At the same location viewed from the same bridge some 23 years later, on 26 September 1986, two decades of lineside maintenance 'holidays' have transformed the once orderly railway into a linear nature reserve, with a

single track penetrating through its heart. Railway operations have also changed beyond recognition, with just one daily freight working to Sharpness now keeping the line open. Although the consist of the train may appear to reflect a buoyant level of business, all the wagons are in fact empties from Stonehouse coal concentration depot and have been tripped to Sharpness simply to enable the locomotive, English Electric Class 37 diesel-electric No 37501, to run round them before returning to Gloucester. *A. Bartlett*

2
Berkeley Loop

A glimpse of a Severn & Wye that might have been: soon after BR's Western Region had taken control of the former LMR main line between Bristol to Gloucester in 1958, the Severn Bridge line was brought into use as a new Sunday diversionary route, not just for the long-established Bristol-Cardiff services, but also, on other occasions, for by-passing the Lydney-Gloucester Central section of the South Wales main line. Hence, on a few such days during the autumn months of 1958, 1959 and 1960, passenger services between Birmingham Snow Hill, Cheltenham and Swansea, then comprising mostly diesel multiple units (DMUs), were routed via the former Midland line from Gloucester Eastgate to Berkeley Road and thence over the Severn Bridge to Lydney. With Berkeley Loop Junction box just visible in the distance, the 10.45am Swansea to Gloucester service, comprising two three-car (later Class 120) Swindon-built 'Cross Country' units, heads towards Berkeley Road over the section of line singled as an economy measure in 1931. The date is 16 October 1960 – just nine days before the event that was to destroy the line's prospects as a diversionary route. *J. Dagley-Morris*

Remotely situated among the fields of Berkeley Vale, with no road or footpath access, Berkeley Loop Junction (1m 26ch) was a Great Western 21-lever signal box set within the 'V' of the junction. Opened by the GWR in 1908, the double-track 1½-mile-long chord made a southward connection into the MR main line at Berkeley

Road South Junction to create an alternative diversionary route to the Severn Tunnel, using GWR running powers over the Midland Railway to Yate. In addition to S&W coal trains from Lydney, the loop also saw limited use by both the GWR and MR for regular freight services. In later years it was only opened for diverted passenger services on certain winter Sundays, and to allow the passage of one or two freight trains each night, the last being the 9.45pm Lydney-Stoke Gifford working on 25 October 1960, which had crossed the Severn Bridge just minutes before its untimely destruction. *M. V. Rees, Coleford Railway Museum*

Looking east, also on 16 October 1960, a Gloucester RC&W-built three-car 'Cross-Country' (later Class 119) DMU, forming the 1.25pm Gloucester to Cardiff service, heads towards Lydney past Berkeley Loop Junction. To the right the loop line sweeps away towards Berkeley Heath to join the former Midland main line at Berkeley Road South Junction. Note that the junction points have recently been renewed with flat-bottom rail, exemplifying the infrastructure investment then being made in this route. *J. Dagley-Morris*

This more typical workaday scene at Berkeley Loop Junction shows the daily Gloucester-Sharpness freight returning from the port with an atomic flask collected en route at Berkeley. The train is in the charge of the usual ex-LMS Fowler 4F 0-6-0, though this one, No 44560, was a bit special, having been one of just five such locomotives originally built for the Somerset & Dorset Joint Railway. By the date of this view, 25 May 1965, the signal box had already been closed in January 1963 and the Berkeley loop lifted. *B. J. Ashworth*

At the south end of the Berkeley Loop was Berkeley Road South Junction, seen here from the west side of the line near the signal box in October 1960, when the loop line was still in use. 'Woofing' its way down the main line southwards to Westerleigh yard with a lengthy mixed freight from Washwood Heath is Saltley depot's ex-LMS 4F 0-6-0 No 44168. *J. Dagley-Morris*

These two further images of Berkeley Road South Junction illustrate steam-hauled diversions working over the Berkeley Loop on Sunday 22 February 1959. Viewed from the signal box is the 8.10am Cardiff-Bristol express, incorrectly headlamped as a stopping passenger service, with Llanelly's ex-GWR 'Mogul' 2-6-0 No 7321 at its head and a six-wheel milk tank at its tail. The driver is carefully observing the 15mph speed limit over the junction where the track is canted in the opposite direction in order to carry high-speed services on the main line. Note the GWR 1 ¼ milepost still in situ just opposite the locomotive. Since closure, the cutting here has been completely infilled and the reclaimed area returned to cultivation. *John Spencer Gilks*

Now looking southwards, this is the 9.00am Bristol–Cardiff express as it slows past the MR's 20-lever box to diverge onto the Berkeley Loop behind one of the more regular performers, ex-GWR 2-6-0 No 6363, of Bristol Bath Road. Other types of latter-day motive power less frequently diagrammed for these services included ex-GWR '2251' Class 0-6-0s and BR Standard '75xx' Class 4-6-0s. During BR days a 15mph speed limit was imposed over the entire 1¼ mile length of the loop line. *John Spencer Gilks*

3
Berkeley Station

After another mile of undulating farmland, the line reached Berkeley station (2m 24ch), rurally situated some three-quarters of a mile from the town it purported to serve. Despite singling of the running line back in 1931, the original Midland Railway goods yard, complete with its substantial red-brick goods shed and weighbridge, remained largely intact until the late 1950s, when the layout was reduced to a single siding accessed from the eastern end only. This rationalisation was to accommodate a very special facility: an overhead gantry crane for the transfer of nuclear waste flasks from two power stations then being built on the Severn

shore at Berkeley and Oldbury. Berkeley Power Station, which opened in 1962, ceased generating in 1989, while Oldbury only operates intermittently and is programmed for early closure. In consequence, operations to serve this facility are at best spasmodic, and rarely amount to more than one train per week. This view, looking westward from Berkeley Ground Frame on 10 April 1997, features a pair of BR Brush Class 31 diesel-electric locos, Nos 31142 and 31512, arriving from Sharpness to collect a waste flask from the siding for onward movement to Sellafield. *A. Bartlett*

From March 1999 all flask train operations on the branch were taken over by Direct Rail Services, a subsidiary of British Nuclear Fuels Ltd, utilising refurbished first-generation diesel locomotives to provide a network of dedicated services throughout the UK. Here, a year later, on 1 March 2000, a pair of DRS's English Electric Class 20 locomotives prepares to depart for Crewe after positioning an empty flask wagon under the gantry ready for loading. *RHM*

The close proximity of the Earl of Berkeley's seat at Berkeley Castle may have prompted the Midland Railway to erect this substantial and stylish station in 1875 before the Sharpness branch became part of the Severn & Wye system. Based on an Italianate design widely used elsewhere on the MR system in the 1870s, the building provided accommodation far superior to anything the S&WR could offer west of the Severn. This is the view glimpsed eastwards from an afternoon service in July 1963. Note the goods shed, then disused but still intact, in the yard beyond. *RHM*

The final view of Berkeley station from the west, on Sunday 9 October 1960, features another diverted service, this time the 9.00am Birmingham Snow Hill to Swansea express, comprised of two Swindon-built 'Cross-Country' (Class 120) DMUs. To the left of this view is the former up-side platform, disused since 1931, while to the right stands part of the former Berkeley Vale Dairy complex, occupied since the late 1940s by road hauliers Western Transport. *J. Dagley-Morris*

4
Sharpness and its dock

After 1 ¼ miles, mostly descending through a shallow cutting at 1 in 200, we arrive at the railway's once impressive approach to Sharpness, Oldminster Junction (3m 45ch), controlled between 1914 and 1965 by the Midland Railway's 24-lever Sharpness South signal box. This is the view north-westwards from an approaching train in March 1964, when the layout was still intact. To the left, the original Midland Railway double-track line continues, as the South Dock branch, for another quarter of a mile to the interchange sidings outside the dock entrance gates. In front of the signal box is the main line to Lydney, and to the right the double-track goods lines that, until 1956, continued as loops serving Oldminster Sidings, before rejoining the main line just south of Sharpness station. *RHM*

Tucked away behind an earth bank opposite Oldminster Junction was the S&WR's only turntable. Hand-operated and with a 45-foot-long deck, it had been installed by the Midland Railway in 1898 for turning the company's small 0-6-0 tender locos, which were then operating daily freight services from Bath, Bristol and Gloucester. Still remembered with disdain by retired Lydney locomen for its stiff and laborious operation, the table was also regularly used until 1950 to turn Lydney-based ex-GWR 'Dean Goods' 0-6-0s working the nightly coal train to Stoke Gifford. When larger GWR '43XX' Class 2-6-0s were allocated to this working, it became necessary to turn them on the Berkeley Road triangle, exposing crews to many miles of tender-first running each

night with just a tarpaulin for protection against the elements. Sharpness turntable nevertheless continued to see regular use by LMR 0-6-0 locomotives working freight trips from Gloucester until the mid 1960s. This view, dating from October 1964, shows its rustic setting and the short connection from the South Dock branch, with a GWR '14XX' tank running past 'wrong line'. Just visible on the right is part of the village of Newtown, which, as its name implies, was developed in the late Victorian era to accommodate many of those employed at Sharpness Dock. *B. J. Ashworth*

Controlling Oldminster Junction from 1914 was this 24-lever Midland Railway box, which was repositioned within the 'V' of the junction and redesignated Sharpness South. The footbridge was of a similar vintage, replacing a potentially dangerous and busy pedestrian crossing, which, at that time, traversed six running lines. The box was decommissioned in May 1965 following official closure of the line to Sharpness station and Severn Bridge some six months earlier. This view dates from September 1950. *R. Carpenter collection*

A glimpse of the interior of Sharpness South box, looking towards Oldminster Junction and showing the standard raised Midland Railway frame with the block shelf above. At the far end of the box is the miniature train staff machine for the 'long' section to Berkeley Road. As was customary in such mechanical boxes, everything is being maintained in immaculate condition. *M. V. Rees, Coleford Railway Museum*

Photographed from an up train opposite Sharpness South box, the fireman is about to surrender the single-line key token for the section from Sharpness station, and to collect a miniature train staff for the 'long' section to Berkeley Road. At times when Berkeley Loop Junction signal box was open and 'switched in', two 'short' single-line sections were created, requiring the provision of one alternative key token for the section from Sharpness South, and another for the section on to Berkeley Road. *G. Stone*

This is Oldminster Junction looking south from the aforementioned long footbridge that provided the principal pedestrian route from Newtown to the dock. In this October 1964 view former GWR 0-4-2T No 1472 is arriving light engine from Gloucester to pick up its auto-trailer at Sharpness station before working the early-evening shuttle service to Berkeley Road. Note that all the goods lines on the left have recently been lifted, although the remainder of the layout is still in full use, including the turntable on the right. Opposite the junction, the small brick building masquerading as a permanent way hut is actually the adapted base of the original MR Oldminster Junction signal box, closed in 1914. *B. J. Ashworth*

This final image of Oldminster Junction, dated 16 October 1964 and looking back towards the signal box and footbridge, features the former Gloucester Barnwood depot's impressively antiquated breakdown train, which includes two vintage ex-Midland Railway coaches. The train is about to return home behind LMS 4F 0-6-0 No 44123 after attending to a minor derailment in the nearby interchange sidings. *B. J. Ashworth*

Returning to the footbridge in April 1964, this is the northward view along the South Dock branch leading to the exchange sidings by the shunters' cabins just visible in the middle distance. With its minimal payload, ex-LMS 4F No 44123 is just setting off with the return working to Gloucester. In the left foreground, beneath the raised bank, lies the platform of the Midland Railway's original temporary passenger station, which was in use for just three years from 1876 until 1879, when the new Severn & Wye & Severn Bridge Railway (S&W&SBR) station opened on the Severn Bridge line. *W. Potter, Kidderminster Railway Museum*

Seen from Pathfinder Tours' 'Severnside Rambler' on 22 April 2007, and looking towards the dock gates, is ex-LMS 'Black Five' 4-6-0 No 45407, the first steam locomotive to visit Sharpness for nearly 42 years. After arriving tender-first from Gloucester, the locomotive is just about to run round its fully booked train of nine coaches. In the background is the support for the loading gauge featured in the following photograph, while beyond are several of the former interchange sidings, still in situ beneath the undergrowth. To the right, the courses of all the former running lines and goods lines to Sharpness station have disappeared beneath a tarmacadamed playground and skate park. *RHM*

Upon dieselisation of all remaining freight services from Gloucester in January 1966, workings to Sharpness were initially entrusted to Swindon-built Class 14 0-6-0 diesel-hydraulic locomotives. Yet by only August of the following year, when this view was captured, the working days of the class on BR were nearly over, most going into long periods of storage before sale to industry or even for scrap. In this view No D9524 is about to depart from the exchange sidings with the return trip to Gloucester New Yard. Exemplifying the increased utilisation made possible by diesel traction, this same locomotive, within its daily diagram, would have already completed an early morning trip to Cinderford and would later continue with another working to Cheltenham. *RHM*

Having now entered British Waterways Board property, with its once extensive 'low level' railway system, the first encounter is with one of the BWB's own dock shunters, No DL2, a 1962-built Andrew Barclay 0-6-0 (works number 3151), seen here in September 1986 with a string of wagons of scrap steel being unloaded at Coopers Metals, on the east side of the dock. Although nearly 20 years have passed since these sidings last saw any regular use, most still remain in situ. *A. Bartlett*

During the last years of railway operations, which finally ceased in the early 1990s, scrap metal for export became the dominant traffic and included many redundant BR wagons that were broken up on site following arrival. Here, on sidings adjacent to Coopers Metals, a batch of ghostly looking china clay 'hood' wagons, already stripped of their timberwork, stand awaiting their fate. *A. Bartlett*

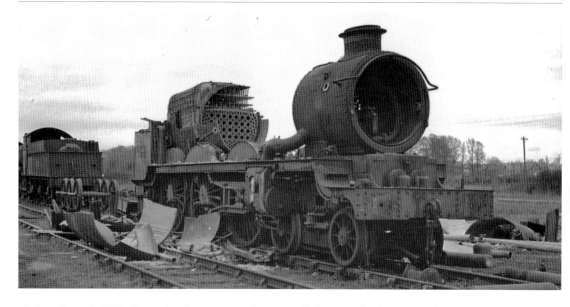

Back in the mid-1960s the market for scrap metal was equally buoyant, leading to the delivery during 1964 of many redundant ex-BR Western Region steam locomotives for breaking up by Coopers Metals. Among several once-prestigious locomotives to be destroyed there was this former Gloucester-based GWR 'Castle' Class locomotive, No 5071 *Spitfire*, which only a few months earlier had been working top-link services to Paddington, including the 'Cheltenham Spa Express'. *Kidderminster Railway Museum*

Sitting forlornly on the quayside in this early 1960s view is the last of the steam shunters to work at Sharpness Dock, Avonside 0-4-0 saddle tank No 1446, built in 1902 and numbered SD3 by the BWB. After the arrival of the diesels in the early 1960s No SD3 was retained as a spare locomotive for three years before succumbing to the cutter's torch – a fate suffered by all its former shedmates. *A. Neale collection*

The ability of Sharpness Dock to accommodate ships of up to 6,000 tons (gross) is evidenced here as the laden Russian freighter *Sonnovisky*, with the aid of a bow line, slowly rounds the knuckle of the north pier to enter the lock at high water. The absence of any tugs to assist with such manoeuvres seems remarkable, especially for vessels such as this, which are not equipped with bow thrusters. Access to the port is difficult at the best of times, being subject to strong tidal currents and, at 34 feet, the second highest tidal range in the world. In this westward view, dating from 5 September 2001, the entrance to Lydney Docks is just visible a mile or so away across the estuary. *RHM*

Turning back the clock to the late 1970s, two London-registered freighters are moored in the capacious tidal basin awaiting high water before sailing away into the evening light. *T. Radway*

Now to the main dock itself, which was opened in 1874 to accommodate the increasing numbers of ever-larger sea-going vessels unable to reach the port of Gloucester by the 1827-built ship canal. Privately owned until 1948 by the Sharpness Docks & Gloucester & Birmingham Navigation Co, the dock was then nationalised and operated by the Docks & Inland Waterways Executive, later the British Waterways Board. In 1997 the entire complex, with the exception of the dry dock, was leased out to Victoria Holdings plc, under whose management the dock has continued to thrive, handling a wide range of mostly imported commodities, including cement, grain, fertilisers and minerals, all now distributed by road via the nearby M5 motorway. In this northward view of the main basin, dating from August 1967, a vintage bunkering tanker, *Britmex No 10*, has just arrived from Port Talbot for repairs in the nearby dry dock. *RHM*

This northward view, dating from June 1966, features one of several Victorian grain warehouses that then still fronted onto the half-mile-long quay wall, while on the extreme right is one of the floating pneumatic grain elevators, which were used to extract bulk grain from ships' holds and discharge direct into lighters or onshore silos. In the foreground, a consignment of West African hardwood logs awaits shipment to Lydney Docks for Pine End plywood factory. *N. Andrews*

This aerial view of Sharpness Dock, looking east, dates from the mid-1970s and shows much of the infrastructure in a state of transition. In a brief clockwise tour, commencing from the tidal basin in the lower right-hand corner, the following features can be identified: the main entrance lock from the River Severn; the dry dock; BWB's diesel loco shed (within the white-roofed building); Dock Row, built in the 1870s to house key members of the Dock Co staff; the 1896-built quay with gantry cranes still in situ; the site of the S&WR hydraulic coal tip; warehouses and cranes fronting onto the 1940s-built west-side quay; extensive stacks of imported timber, virtually all now being distributed by road; the North Dock branch, now lifted; the low-level and high-level bridges; 1890s-built shops and houses (all subsequently demolished by BWB); more timber stacking sheds; the seven-storey North (grain) warehouse; the 1937-built concrete grain silo (replacing an earlier warehouse destroyed by fire); two single-storey warehouses and the seven-storey Albert (grain) warehouse (all now demolished); Coopers Metals scrap-metal yard; and lockside shops, with BWB's former steam loco shed to the rear (all since demolished). Beyond the dock service road and boundary fence at the top of the picture are the BR exchange sidings, still filled with wagons, together with the diesel loco off the daily 'tripper' from Gloucester, with all the former S&W running lines to Sharpness station (just out of the picture, top left), now lifted. *Jet Age Museum, Russell Adams collection*

To accommodate the rapid growth of trade through the port during the late-Victorian era, this additional deep-water quay was constructed in the western corner of the dock in 1896, together with a new single-storey warehouse. The quay was specifically intended to handle general cargoes, most of which required transhipment into railway wagons or barges. To this end, the quay was equipped with one steam crane with a lifting capacity of 30 tons and two lighter cranes, all mounted on travelling gantries. Among the many commodities handled over the years was steel from France for Lydney Tinplate Works, sugar for Cadbury's factory at Frampton, and the export of Forest coal by hoisting up complete railway wagons in slings and discharging their contents into the holds of waiting vessels. This scene, recorded one Saturday in March 1964, shows the quay towards the end of its useful life. In 1976 the cranes, sidings and warehouse were all swept away to enable a new concrete grain silo to be erected on the site. *RHM*

Another facility dating back to the opening of the Sharpness Dock is this dry dock, which is still used intensively to the present day. For many years until the late 1960s it provided a repair and maintenance facility for John Harker & Co, at a time when that company operated many of the oil and petrol tankers on the River Severn. In recent times the dry dock has been leased to Sharpness Shipyard & Dry Dock Ltd, which undertakes work on a wide range of vessels, including, of late, sea-going dredgers, US Army tugs and the MV *Balmoral*. In this April 2007 view, the occupants are *Tirley* and *Chaceley*, both grain barges that latterly worked from Tewkesbury Mill. *RHM*

The dominant feature in this 1955 view of the west side of the dock is the 1908-built hydraulic coal tip, with its reinforced concrete railway viaduct, both of which had replaced earlier timber-framed structures dating from 1886. Originally installed to load deep-draughted vessels and to bunker coal-fired steamers with Forest coal, the tip saw little use after the Second World War, and was eventually decommissioned in the late 1950s. Beyond can be seen the accommodation huts for the National Sea Training School, which was based at Sharpness between 1939 and 1967, while extending from left to right is part of the S&WR's 'high-level' North Dock branch, which also served another smaller coal tip just visible in silhouette against the River Severn. *The Francis Frith Collection, www.francisfrith.com*

Recorded on the western quayside beneath the coal tip viaduct in the early 1970s is the BWB's other diesel shunter, No DL1, a Ruston & Hornsby 0-4-0 (works number 463150) built at Lincoln in 1961. Diesel power had begun to replace steam within the docks in 1961, the previous incumbents comprising three Bristol-built 0-4-0 saddle tanks, two of Avonside lineage and one Peckett. Long after the change-over, the original two-road steam shed adjacent to the lock was closed and the diesels moved to a single-road facility within a new shed adjacent to the dry dock. *T. A. C. Radway*

Until the 1960s shipping activity at Sharpness comprised mostly imports of grain and timber, much of which was transferred to railway wagons or barges for onward movement to Gloucester and the West Midlands. This is the southward view of the dock, as seen from the high-level bridge, showing two coasters transhipping timber from the Baltic ports into lighters for onward movement to Gloucester. Until the Second World War there was no quay wall along the western side of the dock, but with the outbreak of hostilities one was quickly provided, together with a number of electric cranes, several of which are featured here. Note that by the time of this view, August 1967, road rather than rail has become the dominant form of land-borne transport. In the foreground is the original 1875-built low-level swingbridge, which to this day still provides the principal road and (albeit unused) rail access to the west side of the dock. In the distance, the former Severn Mills grain store and warehouse are in the early stages of demolition to make way for further expansion of the then still growing export trade in scrap metal. *RHM*

This westward glimpse over the low-level swingbridge in July 1947 shows the railway set flush into the roadway, with one of the dock shunters waiting to cross to the eastern side. *L. E. Copeland, Wild Swan Publications Ltd*

In 1879, in order to access its coal tips at Sharpness, the Severn & Wye & Severn Bridge Railway was obliged to construct the three-quarter-mile North Dock branch, which included the provision of a substantial swingbridge to cross the north end of the dock. This bridge was designed to accommodate both road and rail access and is still retained in order to provide an alternative roadway to the west side of the dock. Until its closure to rail traffic in 1964 the bridge, which is still hand-operated, was protected on each side by trap points and signals controlled from ground frames. It is remembered by loco crews for its disconcerting bounce when traversed by coal trains from Lydney. This is the road and rail approach as seen from the eastern side in March 1964. *RHM*

Since the end of regular commercial shipping to Gloucester in the 1980s, the high-level bridge has only been opened for the infrequent passage of larger vessels, usually sailing ships en route for repair at Nielsen's yard Gloucester. In 2004, however, for the first time in six years, a German-registered coaster, the *Kormoran*, ventured as far as Hempsted in order to load oil rig equipment for delivery to Norway. This view shows the bridge opened for the vessel as it approaches Sharpness Dock on its return journey on 29 June of that year. *RHM*

One form of waterborne traffic that burgeoned during the 1950s was the movement of oil and petroleum from Avonmouth and Swansea to Gloucester, Worcester and Stourport. In this mid-1950s panorama, taken from the roof of a grain silo, a flotilla of loaded tanker barges is heading northward through the dock, and will bear right to enter the ship canal just beyond the high-level swingbridge. It was two barges such as these that, on the fateful night of 25 October 1960, crashed into and destroyed one of the piers supporting the Severn Railway Bridge, here providing the backdrop, with the Forest of Dean beyond. *Gloucestershire Media*

Silhouetted against the Severn in the previous picture is the S&W&SBR's original 1880-built coal tip. Unlike its larger neighbour in the main dock, this timber-framed and enclosed counter-balanced tip on the old arm remained in almost original condition

and saw regular use until February 1965. Its longevity can be largely attributed to Cadbury's, once a very pro-water transport company, which in 1915 had opened a milk-evaporating factory at Frampton, some 6 miles along the canal towards Gloucester. To power this plant, coal from Forest pits was brought across the Severn Bridge, then tipped into barges for delivery to Cadbury's wharf. Even after the bridge link had been destroyed, the traffic continued, with supplies latterly originating from New Norchard Colliery at Pillowell, then conveyed by road to Princess Royal Colliery before screening and dispatch by rail to Sharpness via Gloucester. The remains of one of the barges once used for this traffic, the *Severn Collier,* now lie among the much-publicised Severnside hulks at nearby Purton. *Kidderminster Railway Museum*

Before leaving Sharpness Dock, there was one further feature of particular interest on the old arm of the ship canal, near where it locked down into the River Severn, for here was moored the training ship *Vindicatrix*. Originally built as a steel sailing ship in 1883, the vessel had enjoyed a remarkably long and colourful service life, before being converted to house most of the communal and teaching accommodation for trainee merchant seamen. Although totally unconnected with the S&W, the National Sea Training School nevertheless generated considerable business for the railway, with around 2,500 cadets attending its courses each year between 1939 and 1967. This traffic even prompted the provision in pre-1960 working timetables of an unadvertised Mondays-only non-stop service from Lydney Junction to Sharpness, albeit with the proviso 'Runs for 10 or more passengers'. This is a 1950s view of the ship looking northwards, with tidal mud flats and the Severn Bridge beyond. Despite an 11th-hour attempt to save *Vindicatrix* for preservation, following relocation of the school to Gravesend, the vessel was broken up at Newport in 1967. *RHM collection*

This final southward view of the S&W&SBR's high-level bridge, with Sharpness Dock beyond, shows two loaded mud hoppers heading towards Purton following dredging operations in the main basin. The low-level bridge can just be seen to be closing behind the second barge. Many of the dockside cranes have been scrapped since this image was recorded in March 2000, while the North warehouse, visible on the left, is now the sole surviving Victorian grain warehouse. *RHM*

Returning to the S&W main line through Sharpness, our next stop is the passenger station (4m 15ch), opened by the Severn & Wye & Severn Bridge Railway in 1879, but also accessed by the Midland Railway. This view, from March 1950, is looking north-west from the adjacent roadway, with the main line from Sharpness South in the foreground, and the North Docks Branch beyond running in across 'Viaduct No 1' above the end of the low-level interchange sidings. The single-storey timber-framed building by the loading dock provided office accommodation for the station master, whose payroll at Sharpness alone still exceeded 30 members of staff at that time. Once again, however, it is the Severn Railway Bridge that dominates the scene. *DFR Museum Trust collection*

The main station building on the up (east) side, was constructed in red brick with a hipped slate roof and a narrow projecting front canopy. With its austere aspect, the building appears to have been very much a 'one-off' design, feigning no allegiance to any established architectural style. Despite the drastic reduction in train services after the Severn Bridge disaster, Sharpness station remained fully manned until final closure on 2 November 1964 – which perhaps accounts in part for the well-kept station gardens. Behind the station in this March 1964 view is the massive three-storey Severn Bridge & Railway Hotel, one of three such establishments to open in the village during the late Victorian era. As at all stations between Berkeley Road and Lydney Town, the LMS was very liberal with the provision of its 'target' nameboards, first introduced in the late 1930s. *RHM*

In 1903, during the early years of joint GWR & Midland Railway management of the line, this most unusual combination of signal box and passenger shelter was constructed by the GWR on the down platform, one new box replacing the two originally provided here when the Severn Bridge line opened in 1879. The replacement 33-lever box remained operational until October 1957, when the main line was singled, the goods lines severed, and control of the North Dock branch junction reduced to a ground frame. This view dates from the early 1950s. *M. E. J. Deane, courtesy of I. Bennett*

One Sunday morning in March 1950 an ex-GWR 'Dean Goods' 0-6-0, No 2322, heads non-stop through Sharpness station with a diverted Bristol to Cardiff express. Until October of that year the very restrictive axle loadings previously imposed by the LMS had severely limited the motive power that could be used over the Severn Bridge. However, following the route's adoption by the Western Region of BR, these restrictions were gradually eased, enabling larger GWR '43XX' 2-6-0s, and later even BR Class 4 4-6-0s, to be used. *W. A. Camwell, courtesy Stephenson Locomotive Society*

At Sharpness station, looking south on a weekday in July 1947, the majority of passengers are clearly railway employees, as they await the imminent arrival of their train to Lydney. At that time, nearly a decade before BR began rationalising the layout, both platforms were in use and the through goods lines to Sharpness South were still operational, as evidenced by the bracket on the Up Starter signal, where they diverged. The 'parachute' water tank at the end of the up platform dated from the 1894-1906 period when the GWR was responsible for maintaining the infrastructure throughout the S&W system. *L. E. Copeland, Wild Swan Publications Ltd*

At the same location some 13 years later, on 16 October 1960, the up side of the station with one running line is intact, but everything else has been stripped away. Heading towards Sharpness South is the diverted Sundays-only 10.45am Swansea to Gloucester service, here formed of two Swindon-built three-car Class 120 'Cross Country' DMUs. *The late R. Dagley-Morris*

Our final southward view of the S&W&SBR station is from beneath the road bridge, showing the extensive cycle storage facilities provided for passengers, many of whom, in pre-car ownership days, had to cycle considerable distances to the station each day in order to reach schools and workplaces from the rural hinterland of Berkeley Vale. *RHM*

This regrettably poor but rare 1940s view northwards from the road bridge adjoining Sharpness station shows the full layout and signalling before rationalisation began in 1956. The North Dock branch, trailing in from the left towards Lydney, was a key part of the original S&W&SBR, enabling train-loads of coal from the Forest of Dean to be routed direct to the sidings serving the Sharpness coal tips. From the mid-1950s all such consignments were normally routed via Sharpness South, where reversal was necessary, followed by hand-over to the dock shunter and a much-extended journey via the low-level dock lines. *S. V. Blencowe collection*

The same viewpoint in 1962 shows the one remaining connection from the North Dock branch, now operated from Sharpness North ground frame, and a new fixed Up Distant installed for Sharpness South. On this occasion the train crew have opted for a few minutes to themselves during their turn-round time, and have run approximately 50 yards north of the station to the end of the post-October 1960 operational line. This was also the location where the auto-trailer was usually stabled on weekdays between morning and evening services – no problems with vandalism in those days! *F. C. Scoon*

Following withdrawal of passenger services on 2 November 1964, the remaining single track through Sharpness station was retained as a siding to the eastern end of the Severn Bridge, which was devoid of any road access. On 13 July 1965 the Western Region's Chief Civil Engineer and a party of Army demolition experts travelled over the line in a BR inspection saloon in order to inspect the bridge. The saloon had worked through as a special train from Reading to Berkeley Road, where it was handed over to the usual 'tripper' locomotive, on this occasion ex-LMS 4F 0-6-0 No 44560. The special is seen here in appalling weather conditions as it negotiates its way over the end of the North Dock branch on the return journey. This manoeuvre, involving a double reversal, was necessary because the running line from the bridge had been severed and slewed to connect into the headshunt off the docks branch. Apologies are proffered for the quality of this image, but its historic significance outweighs other considerations. *D. Markey*

Our final glance back at the S&W&SBR's North Dock branch is from a point just opposite the station yard in 1963, showing both the road and rail access provided over 'Viaduct 1', here traversing low-lying marshland before crossing the north end of the dock by the high-level swingbridge to reach the high-level sidings serving the coal tips. The North Dock branch was officially closed in November 1964 and the track lifted in 1969, while the roadway over Viaduct 1 is now restricted to pedestrian traffic only. *RHM*

5
The Severn Railway Bridge

Just a quarter of a mile beyond Sharpness station, and approached through a deep and sharply curved cutting, was the eastern end of the S&WR's magnum opus, the Severn Railway Bridge. Though built by the nominally independent Severn Bridge Railway, this company immediately amalgamated with the S&WR upon the opening of the bridge to form the Severn & Wye & Severn Bridge Railway. When completed in 1879, the bridge was a phenomenon that set the S&W&SBR apart from almost every other minor railway in Britain, but it soon proved to be a commercial 'white elephant' that would help bring the company's independence to an end within an impressively short space of time.

As with many such ventures in the Victorian era, the bridge project was ultimately the result of a late phase of railway mania based largely upon excessively optimistic forecasts for the continued growth of the Forest coal trade. Its initially successful promotion was based upon two key objectives, driven primarily by the then powerful and influential Forest ironmasters and coal owners: to access the then newly built deep-water port of Sharpness in order to develop the export trade for Forest iron and coal, and second to create an eastward rail route out of the Forest, free from the strictures of the GWR, in order to reach wider markets towards London and the South Coast. That these objective were achieved even to a modest degree was through close collaboration with the Midland Railway, into whose system it physically connected at Sharpness. However, just 15 years later, in 1894, it was a financially exhausted S&W&SBR that was taken over jointly by the GWR and MR.

Fast forward to the late 1940s, and still under the joint management of the GWR and the MR's successor, the LMSR, the Severn Bridge was still fully operational, albeit carrying only modest payloads of coal, freight and local passenger traffic. Since the GWR had opened its loop line at Berkeley in 1908, the company had utilised the route for a limited number of weekday freight services and also, since 1923, for weekend passenger diversions at times when the Severn Tunnel was closed for maintenance.

The bridge led a charmed life, having survived several impacts from errant vessels on the Severn and, during the Second World War, avoided the attentions of the Luftwaffe flying above, and the hazards of the RAF flying below! Its strategic value had also been identified by the GWR during the war, with special contingency arrangements put in place for its use as a diversionary route in the event of the Severn Tunnel being targeted.

In its entirety, the Severn Bridge was 4,162 feet long, and as such was, at the time of its construction, one of the longest iron railway bridges in the UK. Proceeding from east to west, the bridge comprised a 197-foot steam-operated swing bridge across the Gloucester & Sharpness Canal, followed by no fewer than 21 wrought-iron bowstring girders, including two of 312-foot span, all supported on concrete-filled cast-iron piers founded into the river bed of the tidal Severn. It was completed by a curved 12-arch masonry viaduct striding over the western (Forest) foreshore and the GWR's South Wales main line. The entire bridge was built on a rising gradient of 1 in 134 from east to west, and even at high tide the rails were still some 70 feet above the river level where they crossed the navigable channel. A speed limit of 15mph was imposed throughout.

After more than 80 years of underuse, it was a cruel irony of fate, just as the full potential of the bridge was about to be realised, that it should suffer a mortal blow by two tanker barges. Over the ensuing decades, it is not just to the bridge that has been the loser, but also the local railway infrastructure, and the communities it served on both sides of the river.

First impressions: the 197-foot-span, 400-ton swingbridge over the Gloucester & Sharpness Canal is seen here from the east, with the diverted 10.45am Swansea-Gloucester service, comprising two Gloucester RC&W-built three-car 'Cross Country' Class 119 DMUs, about to regain dry land on 16 October 1960. While the swingbridge section was built to accommodate double track, the remainder was for single track only. Power to operate the swing section was provided at any time by one of the duplicate boilers and steam engines installed within the cabin, which was manned by both a signalman and an 'engineman', the latter retained on the Lydney R&M (locomotive) Department payroll. Note the semaphore signal on the swingbridge, positioned at 90 degrees to face oncoming shipping on the canal. *J. Dagley-Morris*

This is the Severn Bridge as viewed from the swingbridge cabin, with an early-morning light engine approaching from Lydney. Although there was no provision for pedestrian access, unofficial arrangements were frequently made between the signalmen at each end of the bridge to enable local inhabitants to cross on foot or with a pedal cycle – usually in the evenings after the last passenger trains had run. *M. V. Rees, Coleford Railway Museum*

These two August 1967 views show the swingbridge in operation, then fully opened for the passage of the Delfzul-registered MV *Tasmanie* heading up the canal towards Gloucester. At times when the bridge was open for the canal, the only access/exit for its operators was via the canal towpath and an internal stairway within the masonry column support. As can be seen, the bridge was designed to swing open anti-clockwise, though there was apparently no locking mechanism to prevent it from turning in the opposite direction. On some unrecorded occasion in the early post-war years, this shortcoming was put to the test by one of its more enterprising operators, with drastic consequences, for while it was still in mid-swing the bridge jammed, rendering it impassable to either rail traffic or shipping. *A. Jarvis*

This was a view of the bridge denied to the public until the advent of diesel multiple units, most of which featured glazed screens behind the driver's cab. This is the prospect from the rear of a westbound diverted service at a point approximately halfway across the bridge in October 1960. Some retired Lydney locomen still delight in relating how, in a strong crosswind, the bridge could clearly be seen to be swaying from side to side. It is perhaps as well that their passengers, ensconced in their snug compartments, were blissfully unaware of this phenomenon, though some of the girders were also inclined to rattle disconcertingly as each train passed by. *S. V. Blencowe collection*

The improbable presence of two ex-GWR 'Castle' Class 4-6-0s on the bridge is explained opposite. They are seen here on one the two massive 312-foot girders that spanned the navigable channel. During the late 1940s and early 1950s the entire bridge underwent a gradual transformation, at the rate of two spans per year, from its old colours of chocolate brown columns and cream girders to an overall shade of metallic grey. Most of this work, at heights of up to 120 feet above the riverbed level, was carried out by BR painters working from timber trestles slung from the girders on ropes and pulleys. *S. V. Blencowe collection*

Castles in the air: on Sundays 15 and 22 July 1956, two of Gloucester Horton Road's ex-GWR 'Castle' Class 4-6-0s, Nos 5018 *St Mawes Castle* and 5042 *Winchester Castle*, took a break from working expresses to Paddington in order to carry out stress and deflection tests on the bridge for the civil engineer. The work was a prelude to the Western Region's plan to upgrade the bridge to carry increased traffic and heavier axle loads, especially at times when the Severn Tunnel was closed for maintenance. Despite its 77-year vintage, the bridge was declared to be fundamentally sound, requiring only upgrading of the diagonal bracings to the girder struts to enable it to fulfil its new role. A contract for this work was subsequently awarded to the Chepstow-based Fairfield Bridge & Shipbuilding Company. Work commenced early in 1960 and continued, despite the damage caused by the barge incident, until all remaining spans had been completed in October of the following year. The 'Castles' are seen here testing the 134-foot span at the western end of the bridge. *Dean Forest Museum Trust collection*

Their work completed for the day, the two 'Castles' head back over the viaduct to Severn Bridge station, before returning home via Lydney and the GWR main line. Some of the engineers' tests also required the 'Castles' to haul a train of loaded ballast wagons over the bridge, but to date no photographs of that operation have come to light. *W.A.Camwell, courtesy of Stephenson Locomotive Society*

With Sharpness providing the backdrop, this is the view of the bridge looking south from a hillside vantage point above the Blakeney road. Just visible on the bridge is a one-coach auto-train, most unusually being propelled towards Lydney. Note that the cast-iron piers supporting the two 312-foot spans over the navigable channel are surrounded with protective timber 'dolphins', unlike the second pier from the left, which was the one subsequently struck and demolished by the tanker barges. *RHM collection*

A brief reminder of the regular post-war formation of passenger trains over the Severn Bridge: ex-GWR 0-4-2T No 1426 rolls sedately across the viaduct with a summer evening return working from Berkeley Road some time in the late 1950s. Both the '14XX' Class locomotives and their GWR compartment-type auto-trailers were introduced onto this service in the late 1930s. From that time onwards, as an economy measure, most of the trains ran without a guard, though all stations along the route continued to be manned. *D. Knight*

This June 1964 view, looking south, features the wide arch spanning the South Wales main line, with ex-GWR 'Grange' Class 4-6-0 No 6859 *Yiewsley Grange* heading past with the 5.45pm stopping passenger service from Cardiff to Gloucester. This was one of many services that reverted to steam traction that year as BR's Western Region wrestled with numerous teething troubles in its new fleet of diesel-hydraulic locomotives. This train was booked to stop at Lydney station for 8 minutes every weekday evening in order to load hundreds of boxes of plastic and rubber products then being manufactured at the nearby industrial estate. *RHM*

The final view of the Severn Bridge when still in operational service was taken from the end of the masonry viaduct on Sunday 21 February 1960, with an approaching six-car Gloucester RC&W-built 'Cross Country' DMU forming the diverted 1.00pm Bristol Temple Meads to Cardiff service. Note the gas main from Gloucester to Lydney, laid over the bridge in 1954, which contributed significantly to the conflagration that followed the tanker accident. For many months after the incident, BR posted one of its employees at Severn Bridge station as a security guard to prevent a constant flow of inquisitive visitors from attempting to walk across the bridge to view the gap. One of these guards proved to be a very affable Welshman who, far from deterring his uninvited guests, was far more inclined, and with only modest encouragement, to give them a well-informed guided tour. *J. Dagley-Morris*

The Severn Bridge disaster and its sequel

The accident that destroyed one of the cast-iron piers and brought down two of the 174-foot spans has been fully chronicled elsewhere, so is only briefly summarised here. On the evening of 25 October 1960 two tanker barges, the *Wastdale H*, loaded with petroleum spit, and the *Arkendale H*, loaded with heavy oil, became lost in a thick fog as they approached Sharpness on a fast incoming tide. Both vessels missed the dock entrance and were swept upstream for a further mile before coming together and colliding with the bridge. In the consequent explosion and fire, which spread across the surface of the river, five of the eight crewmen perished. The two burned-out vessels finished up on the mud bank just to the north of the bridge, where they remain to this day.

Following the incident, British Railways initially made rapid progress in erecting a supplementary trestle to support one of the damaged piers, and prepared design schemes for replacing the missing spans. A flexible gas pipe was even connected up across the gap to maintain supplies to the Forest until a new gas main could be laid from Gloucester. Meanwhile, passenger train services were confined to the Berkeley Road to Sharpness section only, though the 50 or so Lydney Grammar School pupils from Berkeley and Sharpness

continued to travel to school by train; this entailed a daily return journey of nearly 80 miles via Gloucester, using advertised services in the morning, and a non-stop school special in the afternoon.

With covert preparation of the Beeching Plan in full swing by 1962, at some point during that year BR clearly gave up any intention of rebuilding the bridge. The first clear indication of a change in policy was the termination of the school train contract in July, followed by the peremptory closure of the Berkeley Loop in January 1963. Since the loop line carried no regular advertised passenger service, BR was able to implement its demise without any prior public consultation. Formal notices to terminate the Lydney Town-Berkeley Road service were posted following publication of the Beeching Report in March 1963, though the original proposed closure date of 11 November 1963 was deferred by objectors until 2 November 1964.

Demolition of the Severn Bridge proved to be a difficult and protracted exercise that eventually extended over three years. The demolition contract, won by Nordman Construction of Gloucester, entailed the use of a massive floating crane, the *Magnus II*, which was hired from a German company and towed to Sharpness from Hamburg. With a lifting capacity of 400 tons from heights of up to 150 feet, the crane had the capacity to remove each of the bowstring girders complete, except for the two 312-foot spans. Within the three-week period of its hire, commencing on 23 August 1967, *Magnus II* was able to lift and move 16 spans to the shore for cutting and disposal, as well as collapsing the two 312-foot spans into the river and recovering some of the debris for scrap. Not achieved within the programme, however, was the removal of the last three remaining spans, the temporary trestle or the swingbridge. No fewer than 21 cast iron piers had also resisted the crane's attempts to remove them. By engaging sub-contractors, Nordman Construction was able to complete demolition of the viaduct in March 1968, but with many works still outstanding, BR pressing for completion, and a legal dispute over the terms of the crane hire, the company called in the receiver in November 1968 and subsequently went into liquidation. *C. E. Marrows*

After removal from the bridge, most of the still-intact spans were deposited on the west (Forest) foreshore where, between tides, they were cut up, then hoisted up in sections onto the viaduct to be conveyed back to the site of Severn Bridge station for loading onto road vehicles. Direct vehicular access to either foreshore was precluded by the presence of the ex-GWR South Wales main line on the west side, and by the Gloucester & Sharpness Canal on the east. This view shows one of the smaller spans lodged between the end piers of the viaduct, while some of the mangled remains of one of the collapsed 312-foot spans is deposited on the foreshore by *Magnus II*. The absence of any attempt to address matters of public access or safety is quite breathtaking by today's standards, but passed without comment at the time. Although all the iron girders were eventually broken up for scrap, attempts had been made to find a market for them, and at one point it seemed highly probable that some were to be exported to South America. *C. E. Marrows*

After *Magnus II* had returned home, Nordman Construction purchased the Severn King from the Old Passage Ferry, which had ceased to operate in 1966 following the opening of the First Severn Crossing. *Severn King* was then fitted with a crane to salvage scrap metal from the remaining spans and piers for transfer to Sharpness Dock. The former car ferry was also used by a subsequent contractor in connection with the destruction of the pier bases by means of explosives. It was while engaged in this work in July 1969 that a mooring rope parted, resulting in the vessel becoming seriously holed by one of the pier stumps. *Severn King* was quickly salvaged and beached on the foreshore near Sharpness Dock, only to be subsequently broken up. The final stage of the demolition work was the removal of the swingbridge over the Gloucester & Sharpness Canal, the scrap metal being removed by barge. *T.A.C. Radway*

6
Severn Bridge station

Severn Bridge (for Blakeney) station (5m 40ch) is seen here from a steam-hauled Sunday diversion, most probably the 12.57pm from Bristol to Cardiff, slowly approaching over the west end of the viaduct in March 1957. The old Down Home signal on its timber post at the end of the viaduct was one of the very few GWR survivors, installed between 1894 and 1906 when that company was responsible for signalling over the entire S&W system. From the latter date, the Midland Railway and its successor, the LMS, took over the maintenance of all track, signalling and civil engineering works to a point between Travellers Rest and Coleford Junction. *E. T. Gill, R. K Blencowe collection*

Another train taking the long way round, this time it is the 1.45pm Cardiff to Plymouth, comprising eight coaches in the charge of ex-GWR 2-6-0 No 7322, recorded here as it pulls away from Severn Bridge station on Sunday 21 February 1960. In the down platform is one the Lydney-based BR-built 0-6-0 pannier tanks, No 1642, attached to a short permanent way maintenance train, which that day had been making sporadic trips onto the bridge between timetabled services. The timber-framed station buildings, precariously supported on timber posts atop the high embankment, were prefabricated locally by the Gloucester Wagon Co Ltd and delivered in 'flatpack' form for assembly on site. These 'temporary' buildings were destined to provide the principal accommodation at most of the S&WR Co's stations west of the Severn until the lines closed in the 1950s and 1960s. *J. Dagley-Morris*

At Severn Bridge station, the passing loop was controlled by this 1911-vintage Midland Railway 12-lever signal box, seen here in July 1958, freshly repainted in BR WR colours of chocolate and cream. Approaching light engine from Lydney is a '16XX' Class pannier tank, on its way to Sharpness to take up pilot duties on the docks interchange sidings. On the veranda, the signalman is about to collect the single-line tablet from Otters Pool Junction, and to hand over the token for the next section to Sharpness South. After formal closure in 1964, the building was adapted by a local farmer for use as a storage barn, in which guise it survived for nearly another two decades. By 2009, however, the whole station site had become heavily overgrown and was almost unrecognisable as a one-time railway. *R. E. Toop, C. Maggs collection*

Viewed this time from the signal box, the single-line tablet and token are exchanged with the fireman of an up passenger train on 18 July 1958. The usual '14XX' Class locomotive was clearly out of action that day, prompting the use of another member of the '16XX' Class, No 1639, which, not being auto-fitted, would have to run round its train upon arrival at Berkeley Road. The station's claim (partly visible in this view) to be 'for Blakeney' was at best a half-truth, the village of that name lying a full 2 miles away and accessible only through a maze of narrow twisting lanes liberally coated with mud and cow manure. *R. E. Toop, C. Maggs collection*

A down train from Berkeley Road, headed by an unidentified auto-fitted '2021' Class loco, calls in vain for any custom at Severn Bridge station one July afternoon in 1949. At that time all structures both here and elsewhere on the line between Berkeley Road and Travellers Rest (Parkend) were still decorated in the colours of the former LMS. Application of the BR Western Region 'chocolate and cream' colours began the following year. *H. Trigg, R. Barnett collection*

In this final glance back at the remotely situated Severn Bridge station, with the bridge itself beyond, on 18 July 1958, heading towards Lydney is 0-6-0 pannier tank No 1642 with the 1.35pm freight from Sharpness South. This train frequently included wagonloads of newly imported softwood timber for distribution to builders' merchants in the Forest of Dean and South Wales. *R. E. Toop, C. Maggs collection*

From Severn Bridge station the line continued to climb for another quarter of a mile until (at 5m 62ch) it reached the eastern end of Severn Bridge Tunnel. Within the 506-yard-long bore, built to accommodate double track, the line began a 2-mile descent at 1 in 132 to Otters Pool Junction at Lydney. This is the approach to the western portal of the tunnel in May 1962, with its 1874-dated keystone, cast-iron nameplate (now in the DFR Museum), and the LMS fixed Up Distant signal for Severn Bridge station. *RHM*

In June 1964 the Railway Enthusiasts Club of Farnborough chartered two 'Severn Boar' brake-van specials over most of the then-remaining branch lines in the Forest of Dean, each train comprising six assorted vans, hauled over each section by one or two '16XX' Class pannier tanks, Nos 1658 and 1664, which had been specially transferred from Swindon to Gloucester. The second of these tours, on Saturday 20 June, included what was to prove the last passenger-carrying service to reach Severn Bridge station before the line officially closed some 19 weeks later. This is the return working emerging from Severn Bridge Tunnel behind No 1664, complete with express headlamp code and the REC's headboard. *RHM*

7
Lydney Junction

Nearing the once-extensive railway complex at Lydney Junction, the course of the S&W&SBR swings to within 50 yards of the ex-GWR South Wales main line, before running parallel for approximately a quarter of a mile on the approach to Otters Pool Junction. During the early years of the Second World War, various provisions were made to increase the S&W line's capacity as an alternative route to the Severn Tunnel. Among them was a new down loop to hold diverted freight trains off the Severn Bridge line while they awaited a path onto the invariably congested main line to South Wales. Looking east, this view shows the entrance to the loop with the REC's first 'Severn Boar' railtour returning from Severn Bridge behind No 1664 on 7 June 1964. Since 1995 this section of trackbed, opposite Lydney golf course, has lain buried beneath the route of the Lydney Bypass. *RHM*

Looking west from the same spot, some three years earlier on 17 June 1961, an eight-coach excursion from Parkend to Porthcawl has arrived behind ex-GWR '57XX' Class pannier tank No 8701. The locomotive has been uncoupled and another loco, newly attached at the other end, is just drawing the train forward over Otters Pool Junction to commence the main-line stage of its journey. From the mid-1950s until 1961 at least three such excursions ran each summer from Parkend, Whitecroft and Lydney Town, invariably to the same destinations: Barry Island, Porthcawl and Weston-super-Mare. *M. V. Rees, Coleford Railway Museum*

At the quaintly named Otters Pool Junction (7m 71ch) was this replacement signal box installed by the Midland Railway in 1914 to control the short 1879-built East Loop connection from the GWR's South Wales main line. The 22-lever box is seen here, in 1960, with one of its regular operators, Bill Wool (left), and two visiting S&T technicians. Its brick base, here still sporting a 'V for Victory' sign applied some 15 years earlier, was an unusual feature. Although not officially closed until 14 February 1965, the box, together with the running lines to Engine Shed Junction and Lydney Junction, saw no regular use after the autumn of 1961. *M. V. Rees, Coleford Railway Museum*

In this 1960 view from Otters Pool Junction box towards Lydney Junction, signalman Bill Wool is about to hand over the single-line tablet to the fireman of ex-GWR 2-6-0 No 6325 as it approaches over the East Loop connection from the former GWR main line with a train of new 'Dogfish' hoppers loaded with track ballast from Tintern Quarry. For the 2-mile climb from here to Severn Bridge, heavily loaded trains such as this would frequently receive rear-end banking assistance from one of the Lydney-based pannier tanks. *M. V. Rees, Coleford Railway Museum*

Another Sunday diversion, this time the 3.00pm Bristol Temple Meads to Cardiff, comprising two three-car Swindon-built DMUs and a parcels van, threads its way through Otters Pool Junction on Sunday 21 February 1960. The winter of 1959/60 was to prove both the first and last season that these units would operate Bristol-Cardiff services over the bridge. Behind the photographer, the S&W&SBR line continues for another half-mile through Lydney Junction S&W station before joining the original S&WR route at Engine Shed Junction – locations to be visited shortly. *J. Dagley-Morris*

In this glimpse from a southbound main-line train we see the short double-track 'East Loop' connection to the S&W&SBR line. The GWR's massive 84-lever Lydney Junction box, dating from 1904, fills half the picture, with the S&W's diminutive Otters Pool box beyond. This view, looking north-east in about 1963, shows all the track and signalling still in situ though somewhat neglected after many months of disuse. The modern industrial plant providing the backdrop is the then recently opened British Piston Ring Co's foundry, which, despite the scale of its operations, never used the railway. Forty-five years later, the works was still in production under the management of Federal Mogul Ltd, manufacturing castings for the automotive industry. *RHM collection*

Beginning a brief foray onto the main line, we are now opposite the GWR yard foreman's office, to witness the Parkend-Porthcawl excursion setting off behind Lydney-based ex-GWR 2-6-0 No 6394, with a Lydney crew. The locomotive, which has been specially 'bulled up' by the cleaners, was the one normally diagrammed to work the nightly freight service to Stoke Gifford, except at weekends, hence its availability for this Saturday working. In the adjacent loop, at the head of a down freight, is ex-GWR 2-8-0 No 2857, fated to be consigned to Barry scrapyard upon withdrawal, but later rescued for preservation on the Severn Valley Railway. *R. W. Turner*

In March 1969 the main-line layout at Lydney was heavily rationalised, leaving just one up and one down loop off the running lines, together with one crossover and a single connection from the up loop to access the S&W line to Parkend. Lydney Junction signal box was also closed, and Lydney West box reduced to a ground frame to control Station Road level crossing. The simplified layout, including all points (excepting the ground frame-worked S&W connection) and the new colour light signals were henceforward controlled from Newport panel, 25 miles away, through a new relay room located behind the up station platform. This is the barely recognisable site of Lydney Junction looking north-east on 23 April 1994, showing the first main-line railtour to travel over the Dean Forest Railway (DFR) to Norchard Low Level, the Monmouthshire Railway Society's 'Gwaun Cae Gurwen Growler', here rejoining the up loop before reversing back to Chepstow and the land of unpronounceable place names. *RHM*

On 20 July 2002 the Mid Hants Railway ran a special charter train, 'The Gloucester Meteor', from Alton to Lydney (for the DFR) and Newport, hauled throughout by a former Southern Railway locomotive, No 35005 *Canadian Pacific*. Here, with the S&WR's Cookson Terrace in the background and the S&W connection disappearing into the bushes on the right, No 35005 makes an impressively efficient departure on the return journey. Earlier that the day, the outward train had become the first steam-hauled service to call at Lydney station for almost 37 years. *RHM*

Returning to former S&W metals, our journey continues through the once extensive marshalling yard where traffic levels until the late 1950s still required the employment of two shunting locomotives or 'pilots', one at each end of the yard. This early 1964 view, looking south-westwards from a passing train, shows some of the connections between the ex-GWR main line and the S&W. From left to right are two sidings extending back to the GWR station, one of which adjoined a loading bank (still extant) from which Forest coal was once transhipped from the S&W tramroad into broad gauge wagons, then, behind the former GWR yard foreman's office, three former GWR exchange sidings, including the West Loop, which was designated as a through running line. Then there are three more Severn Bridge sidings, two of which extended as loops behind Lydney Junction box to Otters Pool Junction. Further to the right again are three more dead-end sidings, also provided for Severn Bridge line traffic, but latterly used mostly for stabling empty 'pools', ie coal wagons. Finally, on the extreme right, the two running lines of the former S&W&SBR head towards Lydney Junction S&W station, itself just visible above the lines of wagons, with its long connecting footbridge from the GWR station. The entire yard area was developed over drained marshland that 100 years earlier had formed part of a tidal inlet from the nearby Severn estuary. *RHM*

Fast forward to 22 April 2007, by which time most of Lydney Yard had been transferred into the ownership of the Dean Forest Railway. With further rationalisation since BR operations ceased in the late 1980s, just three tracks now remain where once there were nine. In this view, ex-LMS 'Black Five' 4-6-0 No 45407 is about to depart tender-first with the first through passenger train from Lydney to Sharpness – via Gloucester – since July 1962. The train was chartered by Pathfinder Tours, and its organiser, Peter Watts, is seen here attaching the 'Severnside Rambler' headboard. Shortly after leaving Lydney on its 40-mile journey, the train would pass within a mile of its destination! *RHM*

It is midsummer day 1959 as one of Lydney's BR-built lightweight pannier tanks, No 1631, heads northwards through the yard and beneath the lattice steel footbridge linking the former GWR and S&WR stations, both of which were designated 'Lydney Junction' in 1955. To the right, the Lydney works of Wagon Repairs Ltd, which operated on this site from 1924 until 1962, is still busily engaged in helping to maintain BR's then vast fleet of wagons within its modern six-road workshop. During the following year, demountable staging would be introduced within the shops to enable repair and re-roofing works to be safely undertaken on covered vans. *M. V. Rees, Coleford Railway Museum*

The footbridge linking the two stations at Lydney Junction provided an ideal vantage point from which to observe the town's once extensive railway infrastructure, with its almost constant activity. This is the northward view in 1950, showing the dock lines from the left and the S&W yard lines below all converging opposite Lydney Yard box, with the locomotive shed complex beyond and the former S&W&SBR passenger station on the right. Most unusually, the GWR '14XX'-hauled train in the station is made up of main-line corridor stock, possibly because the usual auto-trailers are away at Swindon Works for overhaul. *M. E. J. Deane, courtesy of I. Bennett*

Following the introduction of GWR auto-trains on all Lydney Town to Berkeley Road services in the late 1930s, the only point at which locomotives could take water without incurring delay was on the return journey at the end of the down platform of Lydney Junction S&W station. In this early post-war view, the loco is once again auto-fitted No 2080 (see page 14). Note that the MR water column still features the black and white stripes applied by the LMS during the last war to aid sighting for loco crews during the blackout. *R. K. Blencowe collection*

The same scene is being enacted approximately ten years later, in June 1958. Apart from new coats of paint, the only visible changes are replacement tops to the gas lamps and a new BTC warning sign at the bottom of the ramp. The water supply for the S&WR columns was sourced from the nearby River Lyd, the water being pumped up into two cylindrical storage tanks located above the loco shed roof, then distributed to a total of four columns, two located outside the shed, one at the top of the yard, and one at the west end of the S&W station.
R. E. Toop, C. Maggs collection

This is the former 1879-built S&W&SBR station, looking south-east around the curve towards Otters Pool Junction, in December 1960. The prefabricated timber station building here thriftily incorporated recovered sections from the original S&W terminus, which had been situated adjacent to the GWR station. The shelter on the down side, however, was entirely new. On the right, the ramped access to the 1908-built footbridge can be seen rising behind the station building before turning at 90 degrees to cross a total of 14 tracks to reach the GWR station. At the time of this photograph, BR had thoughtfully renumbered Lydney Junction's four platforms in the following sequence: 2 and 1 (GWR station), followed by 4 and 3 (S&W&SBR station). *RHM*

This view, taken just a few yards away from the one above, and dating from the early months of 1989, provides a sobering reminder of the daunting challenge that confronted the DFR before reconstruction of the station commenced in the early 1990s. Providing a reference point are the rooftops of Great Western Terrace, just visible through the undergrowth on the extreme right. *RHM*

There is no shortage of GWR auto-trailers in this 1951 westward view of the S&W&SBR station, still largely in its original condition, except for the replacement LMS station nameboards erected in the late 1930s, and a GWR running-in board inviting passengers to 'change for South Wales, Paddington and the Great Western Line'. Beyond the railway yards, the industrial backdrop is provided by Lydney Tinplate Works and the locomotive depot. *R. S. Carpenter collection*

The same location is barely recognisable some 47 years later, in September 1998, despite the presence of a new replica station building and running-in board. This is the DFR's Lydney Junction S&W station in its initial guise, following reopening on 2 June 1995, with the original down-side platform now extended westwards, and backed by a temporary fence, pending completion of a second platform to form an island. As in so many other locations, the previously open aspect of the railway has been completely transformed by the unfettered growth of trees and shrubs over the previous 30 years. Visiting GWR auto-fitted pannier tank No 6412 waits in the loop to take the next passenger train to Norchard, while in the yard beyond No 9642 is assembling a demonstration freight for Parkend. *RHM*

Business still appears buoyant in this March 1964 vista from the footbridge looking eastwards across the S&W yard towards Lydney Junction box and the South Wales main line, where a down freight is passing by. By this time Lydney Yard was also being used as the holding and collection point for block trains of track ballast from Tintern Quarry, as evidenced by the many 'Dogfish' ballast hopper wagons prominent in this view. *F. A. Blencowe*

These two views show the former Wagon Repairs workshops, the first taken from the footbridge shortly after closure, and the second from the GWR station some two years later. From the elevated view can be seen the wagon traversers that were located at both ends of the shops. Latterly all wagon movements in and around the works were carried out by specially designed rubber-tyred tractors fitted with buffing plates and couplings. The rapid reduction of BR's wagon fleet and the demise of most timber-framed vehicles in the early 1960s hastened the closure of many such works at that time. During most of the 1970s the site was occupied by scrap merchant LMC Metals Ltd, which consigned some of its scrap steel by rail. All the workshops were demolished during that firm's tenure of the site, which since 1990 has been occupied by the London Bus Export Co. *S. V. Blencowe*

Lydney (GWR) station

The former Great Western Railway main-line station, known simply as Lydney until 1955, and again so since 1968, dates back to 1851, when this section of Brunel's broad gauge South Wales Railway was initially opened from Grange Court to Chepstow East. Upon completion of the Wye Bridge at Chepstow, it became a through route to Cardiff the following year, and was subsequently converted to standard gauge in 1872. Until the Severn Tunnel opened in 1886, this was the GWR's principal route from London to South Wales, and still becomes so whenever the tunnel is closed for maintenance.

Given the GWR's status, and the potential business on offer in the 1850s, the original facilities provided at Lydney were remarkably modest, comprising a Brunel chalet-style building constructed in a dour grey Forest sandstone with slated roof. In the adjacent goods yard on the down (southbound) side there was but one siding and a timber-framed goods shed to serve the town, while on the up side there were three interchange sidings with the S&WR and two sidings opposite the original S&W tramroad coal tips. Much of the Victorian infrastructure remained in place until after the Second World War, although both of the earlier signal boxes at Lydney Junction and Lydney West had been renewed by the GWR in 1904 and 1918 respectively, while additional up and down goods loops were added during the 1940s.

From 2 November 1964, closures under the Beeching Plan left Lydney as the only passenger station between Gloucester and Chepstow. Over the ensuing years of the decade, the ruthless enforced run-down continued, with parcels and sundries being withdrawn at the end of 1965, the former GWR goods depot closing completely in 1967, and the station becoming unstaffed in October 1969. Furthermore, in the summer of that year, under Harold Wilson's Labour Government, BR unexpectedly posted notices proposing complete closure of Lydney and Caldicot stations and the reduction of passenger services at Chepstow to but a token level. However, following a poorly prepared case by BR and strong representations from both Caldicot and Chepstow, closure was narrowly averted. Thus, 40 years on, it is largely thanks to its neighbours west of the River Wye that Lydney still enjoys a regular train service.

Lydney's former GWR station was, with its original Brunelian buildings, still largely intact, albeit with the later additions of station master's office, platform canopy and gents' toilet on the up side, and a modern brick-built office in the goods yard. This is a westward view of the station in June 1958, with vintage ex-GWR 2-6-0 No 5398 passing through with an up freight. Note that the running-in board, which until about 1950 had entreated passengers to 'Change for the Severn & Wye Railway', has been amended by BR to more helpfully identify two of the destinations that could still be reached by that line. *R. E. Toop, C. Maggs collection*

Opposite top: **In another westward view of the station on 29 October 1961 a Sunday diversion, the 6.45am Fishguard Harbour to Paddington, coasts through behind ex-GWR 'Castle' Class locomotive No 5062 *Earl of Shaftesbury*. The typical smart turn-out of this Swansea Landore locomotive, with its silver-painted buffers, was attributable to the depot's former shedmaster, Roy White, who had commenced his railway career as an engine cleaner at Lydney back in 1934. Note that the brass beading on the loco's rear splasher is coming adrift. *RHM***

Opposite bottom: **By contrast, at the same location some 45 years later the West signal box and down-side waiting room (now with flat roof) are the only surviving buildings from the steam age. On the up side Brunel's old station, with all its offices, waiting rooms and toilets, has been swept away and replaced by a mean concrete shelter quite unworthy of the town it serves and patently inadequate for its purpose. Slowly entering the station on 18 July 2006 is a specially chartered 'Heartland Tours' train for Gloucestershire protestors travelling to London to make representations at the Houses of Parliament regarding proposed swingeing cut-backs to NHS services in the county. The train, which was hauled by Cotswold Rail's Class 47 diesel-electric No 47813, was fully booked and, largely as a result of the day's actions, many of the targeted facilities – including Lydney Hospital – were saved from closure. *RHM***

Above: **As a further contrast, recorded on the down line in April 1961 is a not unusual phenomenon from the pre-motorway age: a brand-new diesel-hydraulic 0-6-0 shunter, No RTB 1, nearing the end of its 175-mile delivery by rail from the Yorkshire Engine Co's works near Sheffield to the soon-to-open steelworks of Richard, Thomas & Baldwin at Llanwern. Behind the down platform the former GWR goods yard is still very active, with deliveries of grain, animal feeds and fertilisers to its many regular customers, including Lydney Farmers Stores and Bathurst Park Estate. At that time at least four road delivery vehicles were required to service the depot. *RHM***

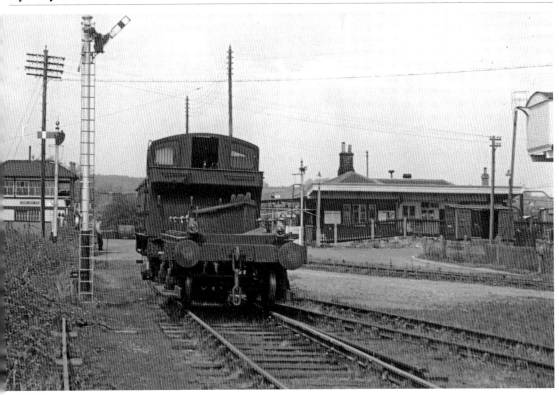

Opposite top: **It was at the west end of the GWR station that its most interesting feature was to be found: the 90-degree flat crossing of the GWR main line by the original S&WR's 'main line' from Lydney Yard to the docks, controlled by the adjacent Lydney West box (25 levers). The S&W had already opened its tramroad to the Upper Basin (in 1813), long before Brunel's South Wales Railway came upon the scene in 1851. Over the ensuing 21 years every permutation of tramroad, broad gauge and standard gauge crossing evolved, until standard gauge was adopted by both railway companies, although the S&WR also retained a tramroad crossing until 1880. This is the improbable scene from the west end of the up platform on 8 June 1962 as Lydney's S&W yard pilot No 1650, with its shunters' gig still branded 'Lydney (S&W Joint)' cautiously propels its train across the former GWR main line towards the docks.** *The late R. Dagley-Morris*

Opposite bottom: **In this southward view, taken on 22 June 1959 from the boarded crossing between Station Road and the GWR station, Lydney's S&W yard pilot No 1627 is returning from the docks with a string of empty seven-plank coal wagons and is about to cross the GWR main line. Two sets of wheel-operated gates were installed here: one for the road level crossing, and the other for the dock line gate. All approaches to the crossing from the S&W dock lines were protected by catch points and semaphore signals worked from the West box – an arrangement initially resisted by the S&WR Co many years before, after it had become the custom for its shunting locos to be simply 'waved across' the South Wales main line!** *M. V. Rees, Coleford Railway Museum*

Above: **Lydney's former GWR station is seen on 4 May 1962 from the Lower Docks branch, where pilot loco No 1608 is awaiting a path over the main line back to the S&W yard. On the left is Lydney West signal box, unusually constructed directly over a cattle creep, while adjacent is the level crossing with Station Road, which here makes a tortuous Z-bend across and around the S&W lines on its way to the docks. The SWR's original 1851 station building is on the right, complete with its later GWR canopy, and a crude scaffold-framed shelter erected by BR to provide cover for the then bourgeoning parcels traffic. Finally, just visible on the extreme right is the former GWR water tower, located within one of the rear gardens of Great Western Terrace, which supplied the company's four water columns located adjacent to the main line. Despite endeavours by the nascent DFRPS to lease the recently vacated station in 1970, BR responded by demolishing the building shortly afterwards. Had it been able to survive for but a few more years, Brunel's station would almost certainly now be a listed building with an assured future – as is now the case at neighbouring Chepstow.** *RHM*

8
Lydney Docks

Just yards beyond its flat crossing of the South Wales main line, the S&WR dock line divided at Upper Dock Junction (8m 60ch). In this view, looking south-east in May 1962, the Upper Docks branch is bearing sharply away to the left to the north side of the canal and the Pine End plywood factory, while on the right is the Lower Docks branch, on which S&W pilot No 1608 still stands awaiting a path across the main line to Lydney Yard. *RHM*

Veering left onto the Upper Docks branch, the single line passed in front of two groups of railway houses: Great Western Terrace, one of that company's standard red-brick, slate-roofed designs, dating from the 1890s, and the S&WR's highly distinctive Cookson Terrace, built in 1859 and named after its one-time Chairman. The latter row, finely constructed in Forest stone with steep slate-clad gables, also incorporated the three-storey Railway Hotel as its centrepiece until 1970.

As well as housing many key S&WR employees, the terrace had also formerly accommodated a Post Office, a customs office and commercial offices for coal factors exporting from the docks. This north-westerly view from the railway in the mid-1950s also shows the traffic lights installed during the Second World War to control the single-lane section of roadway that ran parallel with the branch for some 300 yards. Fifty-five years later, both the terraces are still occupied, while the S&W building also now enjoys Grade 2 listed status. *I. Thomas, Forest Prints*

This is the opposite end of the single-lane section of Harbour Road, looking back towards Lydney Junction, and showing the unfenced Upper Docks branch sweeping around the site of a recently lifted raft of sidings that had formerly served two long-closed coal tips on the north side of the Upper Basin, itself just visible on the left. On 6 July 1962 an Austin A40 Somerset passes S&W pilot No 1650 on its return trip from Pine End. Note the two shunters, enjoying a comfortable but unauthorised ride atop their wagon on this warm summer's day. Since closure of the railway, the road has been widened and a small trading estate now occupies the site of the sidings. *RHM*

Until 1941 the Upper Docks branch terminated alongside the canal, at a point where the Pine End extension subsequently crossed Harbour Road at an acute angle (9m 16ch). Here, as No 1650 heads back to Lydney Yard with its short train, the formality of deploying flagmen has been dispensed with; instead, the tactic is simply to wait for a gap in the traffic and make a dash for it. Beyond the train, the cranes of Pine End are already looming large on the horizon. *RHM*

Viewed from the opposite side of the canal on 16 July 1962, the S&W pilot is seen here cautiously propelling empty vans through the Pine End factory gates and onto the two sidings at the end of the branch (9m 50ch). The locomotive is just clearing the main entrance to Lydney Industrial Estate, then being developed on the site of the former Ministry of Supply depot occupied by the US Army during the war as a salvage and distribution depot, and independently served by sidings off the GWR main line. To the right are the massive gantry and cranes where, during the post-war years, hardwood logs from West Africa were offloaded from barges for stacking before being processed into marine plywood and veneers in the adjacent factory. Pine End works had originally been established by the Ministry of Supply in 1941 as a shadow factory to manufacture plywood for wartime use, including panels for Mosquito fighter-bombers and troop gliders. Latterly, inward rail traffic comprised mostly domestic hardwood tree trunks for conversion into veneers, and manufactured goods dispatched in covered vans. The Upper Docks branch was closed by BR in August 1963, and all trackwork was lifted within a month. *RHM*

Opposite: These two further views of Pine End are again from the opposite side of the canal, showing the final water-borne consignment of hardwood logs in 1982. Unlike most previous deliveries from Avonmouth, which had ceased some five years earlier, this final trial load had been transhipped at Sharpness and ferried across the Severn in three motorised barges operated by F. A. Ashmead & Sons. Having developed at one point into the largest plywood factory in the UK, changing world markets subsequently led owners Mallinson Denny to diversify its product range. Eventually, following a management buy-out, the works ceased production altogether in 2004. Five years later, the entire 14-acre complex, which had once employed 600 workers, was still empty and awaiting redevelopment. *G. Caldwell*

We now turn our attention to the Lower Docks branch. Accessed from a siding off the branch adjacent to Upper Docks Junction, this was the S&W company's 1813-built dock office and warehouse, located at the head of the Upper Basin. The building fell out of use during the 1950s but has somehow managed to survive into the 21st century, albeit in a much modernised and barely recognisable form. It is seen here in the late 1960s at the low point of its fortunes. Visible beyond are the bases of former coal tips Nos 1 & 2. *S. V. Blencowe*

Approximately 150 yards south of Upper Dock Junction, the Lower Docks branch crossed the River Lyd on a hand-operated swingbridge, latterly protected on both sides by LMS semaphore signals. The bridge had been required to swing in order to permit vessels to reach the nearby Tinplate Wharf, itself connected to Lydney Tinplate Works by means of a narrow gauge tramway worked by horse power until shipments finally ceased the late 1930s. This view once again features S&W pilot No 1650 as it slowly propels its train over the bridge on 8 June 1962. The ruins of the former transfer shed on the Tinplate Wharf can just be seen to the right. Immediately beyond the swingbridge the branch crossed over an extension of the tramway leading to a further canalside wharf, before passing three fans of derelict sidings that had formerly served coal tips Nos 3, 4 and 5, on the south side of the Upper Basin. After closure of the Lower Docks branch in November 1960, the top end was adapted to form a service road to a new sewage works, while the remaining 1¼ miles to the Lower Basin has since been designated as a public footpath. *J. Dagley-Morris*

After pursuing a straight and level course along the top of the canal bank for nearly a mile, the Lower Docks branch opened out into a further fan of nine sidings, which until the 1950s continued to serve two coal tips, Nos 6 and 7, both situated on the south side of the Lower Basin. Opposite these sidings a swingbridge, which once carried one of the S&WR's tramroads across the canal, remains in use to this day. Just beyond the bridge, on the north side of the canal, stood the imposing detached residence of Lydney's Harbour Master – until about 1970, that is, when it too became another victim of BR's 'scorched earth' policy. This is a 1930s view, which remained virtually unchanged until the early post-war years, looking east, featuring the Harbour Master's house and the now Grade 2 listed swingbridge, with a fascinating selection of vessels moored in the Lower Basin beyond. The two coal tips on the south side of the basin are just out of view on the right. *Dean Heritage Museum Trust*

As ever, British Railways wasted no time in destroying the infrastructure and lifting the tracks following the last shipment of coal on 31 October 1960, and formal closure of the branch on 18 November. Less than four months later, demolition of tip No7 can be seen to be well under way, while No 6 has already gone. Like all its neighbours, No 7 was of a timber-framed, counter-balanced design, and had been erected by the Midland Railway some 50 years earlier to replace a life-expired S&WR structure. This view also shows the small turntable onto which loaded wagons were manoeuvred before being propelled onto the tip. All such wagon movements were accomplished by hand, albeit aided by gravity, since all sidings for loaded wagons were graded down towards the turntable, and the one for empties away from it. Apart from manhandling loaded wagons weighing up to 17 tons gross (many still with grease axleboxes), the loaders also had to cope with harsh weather conditions, for this elevated location was exposed to the full force of south-westerly gales and storms blowing up the Severn estuary. Providing the background to this west-facing view are the tramroad swingbridge and the Harbour Master's House, with Pine End works beyond. *RHM*

Viewed from the north side of the Lower Basin in happier times, a decade or so earlier, a long-time regular visitor to Lydney, the de-rigged and motorised Severn Trow *Jonadab*, slowly makes its way past tips Nos 6 and 7. Like many such craft working the Severn at that time, the *Jonadab* was of an impressive vintage, having been built as a sailing vessel way back in 1848, and motorised exactly a century later, eventually ending its days as a beached hulk just a few hundred yards away to help protect the south side of the Lower Dock branch embankment from erosion by the River Severn. *Dean Heritage Museum Trust*

At its eastern end (9m 72ch), the Lower Docks branch terminated abruptly at a wagon turntable serving coal tip No 9. This was located opposite the Tidal Basin, next to the lock gates giving access into the Severn, and was both the most intensively used, and the last to remain in operation. It is seen here in action in 1959, loading the Chester-registered *Carita*, a former John Summers vessel that by this time was operating from Appledore. One aspect of such operations rarely captured, but clearly evident here, was the voluminous clouds of dust and grit that erupted each time an avalanche of coal descended into the hold, so much so that, in the days of coal shipments, the Lydney sands were always heavily streaked with shades of black and grey. *M. V. Rees, Coleford Railway Museum*

Until the early 1950s the S&WR's old steam dredger and four barges were maintained at Lydney for clearing the basins and the canal, all arisings being deposited into the Severn by means of a steam crane positioned over the weir adjoining the Lower Basin. After nationalisation, all such operations were subsequently taken over by the British Waterways Board, utilising a dredger and mud hoppers brought across the river from Purton, near Sharpness. Seen here in Lydney's Tidal Basin in April 1962 is the BWB steam dredger No 4, built in Holland in 1925 for the Sharpness New Dock Co and now preserved at the National Waterways Museum at Gloucester. *RHM*

Right up to the mid-1950s one or two fully rigged sailing vessels continued to trade at Lydney. Among them was the *Eilian*, a three-masted schooner dating from 1908, which was owned and operated by a Braunton family, and frequently loaded with Forest coal for use at Ilfracombe gas works. The vessel is recorded as having made 330 visits to the Forest port before being sold on to a Norwegian owner in 1957. It is seen here moored under No 9 tip. On the opposite side of the Tidal Basin the *Jonadab* and another vessel are already loaded and waiting to leave at high water. *Dean Heritage Museum Trust*

This is the Tidal Basin on 5 November 1960, just five days after the last shipment of coal, with the last train of empty wagons still awaiting collection. In Victorian times, gas lighting had been installed on all the tip lines on the west side of the canal to facilitate night-time working, but only tips Nos 6, 7 and 9, and the Tidal Basin and pier were later provided – albeit sparingly – with electric lighting. Empty barges *Hanham* and *Dursley* have been brought down from Pine End to await collection by the Avonmouth tug. *RHM*

Viewed from No 9 tip, this is a typical delivery of logs for Pine End arriving from Avonmouth Dock at high water on 28 October 1961. The tug is the steam-powered *Sea Gem*, towing two unpowered dumb barges, *Seend* and *Twerton*. Even in favourable conditions, each 21-mile leg of this round trip would take at least 1 ½ hours, during which time the lightermen would have to steer their vessels in all weathers while standing on a small and completely unprotected stern counter. Entry into Lydney Harbour was invariably a tricky exercise, requiring vessels to swing round through 180 degrees to face the running tide and maintain steerage way before rounding the pier and entering the lock. Whenever possible, the crew

bringing up a train of loaded barges from Avonmouth would endeavour to take the empties back on the same tide, calling for a slick turn-round during the few short minutes of slack water at high tide. *RHM*

Our visit to Lydney Docks ends on a high note, for despite all the previous decades of run-downs and closures, the historic value of the lower docks was finally recognised in 1980, when the entire area encompassing the Lower Basin, the Tidal Basin and the pier was designated as a Scheduled Ancient Monument. This act, in theory at least, has bestowed upon the dock a legally protected status against any further damage or predations. Not only has the site now been secured for the future but, since 2002, no less than £1.9 million has been invested there by the Environment Agency, aided by a 75% grant from the Heritage Lottery Fund. Principal works have included conservation of the dock's historic fabric, replacement of lock gates, incorporation of a flood barrier against the high spring tides, and provision of mooring facilities for 50 boats. Throughout all the years of uncertainty the Lydney Yacht Club has retained its club house in one of the few remaining buildings opposite the Tidal Basin, and through its ongoing presence and publicity has gradually helped to raise to the profile of the docks. The net result is that all moorings in the Lower Basin are now fully subscribed, and the dock has once again become a focal point of interest to both locals and visitors alike. And, as if to provide the icing on the cake, the MV *Balmoral* has, since 1991, continued to call at Lydney at least two or three times each year to take 200-300 passengers on day-long cruises to Bristol Channel ports and piers as far as Ilfracombe. Here, the classic profile of the ship is captured against the morning light as it slowly manoeuvres against the incoming tide to berth alongside the pier. *RHM*

9
Lydney Yard and Shed

Returning to Lydney's former GWR station, here is S&W pilot No 1650 again, now propelling its train from the S&W yard towards the flat crossing over the main line on 8 June 1961. The short spur alongside the loco. had once extended over the flat crossing as a second line to the docks, but long before the 1950s had been used for loading the daily S&W sundries (parcels) van at the rudimentary platform before its attachment to the Coleford goods. In the foreground the wrought-iron fencing marks the top of a ramp from a subway constructed by the S&WR in 1875 to provide pedestrian access from Station Road, beneath the dock lines, to its original terminal station, which was located to the rear of the GWR station. Although a new through station was opened on the Severn Bridge line just four years later, in 1879, the old subway remained in use until the mid-1960s. *The late R. Dagley-Morris*

On the site of the former S&WR terminus, adjacent to the docks lines, were five carriage sidings, all covered until 1924 by a large iron-framed shed adapted by the S&WR from a former church building – complete with its stained glass windows! By 1950, when this photo was taken, the shed had long gone, but the sidings were still in use for stabling coaches and for undertaking wagon repairs. Prominent against the stopblocks are two of the GWR's 1930s compartment-type Brake 3rd auto-trailer coaches, then still sporting chocolate and cream livery. Until the Severn Bridge route was severed, five of these trailers were based at Lydney, all branded 'To work between Lydney Town & Berkeley Road'. By the late 1950s they were usually stabled either at the rear of the S&W Junction station, or on the former permanent way engineer's siding near the locomotive shed. *E. J. Deane, courtesy of I. Bennett*

On Sunday 8 September 1963, barely four weeks after the closure of the Pine End branch, the flat crossing is no more. This is the view looking northwards from Lydney GWR station along the S&W dock lines towards Lydney Yard, with the just-recovered crossing timbers being held aloft like a trophy. Beyond, the up and down dock lines are about to be truncated at a point just beyond the pedestrian subway, while all the point rodding and signals have already been dismantled ready for removal. For more than 100 years, until just the previous day, the distinctive rhythm of main-line trains hammering over this crossing was one that could be clearly heard a mile away in the town centre. *RHM*

The uninviting subway entrance from Station Road to the S&WR's original station at Lydney Junction is seen here while in the process of being infilled after the dock lines had been closed. *F. A. Blencowe*

In April 1997 the embankment carrying the former S&W dock lines has been swept away to create the alignment for the new spine road between the station and the Lydney Bypass. The new road, with its level crossing over the DFR's S&W line, was officially opened on 15 May 1997. *RHM*

Until 28 June 1960 Lydney Yard signal box (8m 19ch) controlled all movements within the former S&W yards, including the junction with the docks branch and a direct connection from the West Loop onto the adjacent S&W down line for goods and mineral trains departing for the Forest. This is the former 16-lever box, erected by the Midland Railway in 1919, still fully operational but long overdue for a new coat of paint in September 1950. The adjoining building accommodated the S&W yard foreman's office, together with a mess room for guards and shunters. Note the strategically placed re-railing ramp leaning against the end of the box – it would see plenty of use over the ensuing decade. *W. A. Camwell, courtesy of Stephenson Locomotive Society*

These two photographs were taken from almost the same vantage point. Over a period of some three months in the spring of 1967 the bitumen distribution depot operated by Berry Wiggins & Co at Whimsey, near Cinderford, since 1949 was relocated piecemeal onto the site of the former dock lines and carriage sidings at Lydney Junction. The new depot comprised three sidings serving two rows of bitumen and the storage tanks, all heated (to maintain fluidity) from oil-fired boilers located at the northern end of the site. The site generated a regular inward traffic of around eight loaded four-wheeled tank wagons each weekday, plus further vehicles to deliver the heating oil, all conveyed from the company's own refinery at Kingsnorth on the Hoo peninsula in Kent. Onward distribution from Lydney was by road tankers, some of which were owned by Berry Wiggins and some by private contractors. After barely four years of operation, the depot relocated again to Cardiff, and all plant was subsequently cut up on site by scrap merchant LMC Metals Ltd, which by then was occupying the adjacent Wagon Repairs site. This is the Berry Wiggins depot, as viewed from the north on Sunday 26 April 1970, when a DFRPS walk of the S&W line, organised by the BR Area Manager, coincided with the arrival of WR 'Warship' Class diesel-hydraulic No 852 *Tenacious* with empty ballast hoppers. *RHM*

Fast forward 37 years, we see a completely transformed scene on 22 April 2007. On the left is the S&W station, completely rebuilt by the DFR and opened on 2 June 1995, with an island platform extended to accommodate incoming trains from the main line – a use to which it is being tested here for the first time. In the centre, the DFR's restored GWR '57XX' pannier tank No 9681 is setting off for Parkend with Pathfinder Tours' 'Severnside Rambler', which has just arrived from Gloucester behind ex-LMS 'Black Five' 4-6-0 No 45407. *RHM*

Sunset on the old order at Lydney Yard: this final southward view shows the S&W&SBR station on the left, the substantial MR-built yard foreman's office in the centre, and the truncated docks lines running straight ahead towards Lydney West box, itself just visible to the right of the brake-van. The WR '16XX' yard pilot, No 1631, was the last of its class to work from Lydney shed, which closed the day after this scene was recorded on 28 February 1964. In the left foreground the masonry parapet locates the point where the S&WR crosses the River Lyd, from whence water was pumped to twin storage tanks above the locomotive depot. *RHM*

After nearly 30 years of declining use and neglect, the scene was transformed by the DFR in the mid-1990s. New tracks were laid into the S&W Junction station and into the yard, all controlled from Lydney Junction S&W signal box (8m 21ch), a 1950s-vintage 35-lever BR LMR example recovered from Heysham, Lancashire. Built to control a new level crossing for the re-routed Station Road, the box was commissioned in October 1996. This view, also looking south from a point opposite the former locomotive sheds in March 1998, illustrates another phenomenon never anticipated by the Victorian railway companies, or indeed by the early preservationists: 'Thomas the Tank Engine', here seen with the DFR's Hunslet 0-6-0 saddle tank Wilbert, itself named after the author of the 'Thomas' books, the late Reverend Awdry, one-time President of the DFR. The line in the foreground provides the DFR's road-to-rail offloading point, and also accesses two sidings that, since the summer of 2000, have become the restoration and operational base for the Dean Forest Diesel Association. *RHM*

Looking north from a point adjacent to the new signal box in October 1997, resident GWR 'small Prairie' 2-6-2 tank loco No 5541 and visiting GWR pannier tank No 7754 negotiate the new track layout under the control of refurbished signals salvaged from Corby, Northamptonshire. *RHM*

Situated on the down (west) side of line, at the north of Lydney Yard, the S&WR's loco shed had been established on this site as far back as 1865 when the first tramroad locomotives arrived. Over the ensuing 30 years the buildings were successively enlarged and adapted to accommodate first broad gauge then standard gauge locomotives, with a three-road running shed and a one-road repair shop. The enlarged complex, with its Forest stone walls, timber-clad gables and slated roofs, also housed a machine shop and stores, though these areas were subsequently adapted for use by the civil engineer. Later additions included a separate brick-built office and stores building fronting onto Church Road, and a new sand-drying house. The former Midland Railway coach body on the left accommodated staff lockers and cycles, while the building behind No 1630 housed the loco crews' mess room. Gas lighting prevailed to the end. *C. H. Townley, courtesy of Industrial Railway Society*

This view, taken 12 years later on a dour November day in 1963, features a most improbable line-up outside the shed, including two outsized visitors, ex-GWR 4-6-0s Nos 5979 Cruckton Hall and 6879 Overton Grange. The rare appearance of such main-line locos was invariably to power heavy ballast trains from Lydney Yard at weekends to wherever track renewal works were taking place on the Western Region. Note that the gable-end of the shed has been re-clad with asbestos cement sheeting following re-roofing with the same material. On the right are the 1890-built offices and stores and the coal-fired sand dryer dating from 1910. *RHM*

Looking north from the shed in 1950, this is the coal-loading bank, upon which a hand-operated hoist had previously been available to replenish bunkers and tenders. Latterly, all coaling was by hand. This view shows two generations of S&W motive power on the adjoining ash pit road. On the left is one of the GWR's '2021' Class of lightweight pannier tanks, which had worked S&W line services since the earliest days of GWR & MR joint ownership in the 1890s, while on the right is No 1612, one of the first of their new replacements to arrive from Swindon Works in 1949. Beyond the locos can be glimpsed Lydney's breakdown train on the left, and Engine Shed Junction signal box on the right. *M. E. J. Deane, courtesy of I. Bennett*

Taken in about 1951, this photograph looking eastward across the shed yard features two more recently delivered '16XX' Class pannier tanks, Nos 1631 and 1632. Beyond the tracks lies the East Marsh, and beyond that the S&W&SBR line and Severn Bridge sidings sweeping back towards Otters Pool Junction after completing a 150-degree arc through Lydney Junction station. *M. E. J. Deane, courtesy of I. Bennett*

In Lydney shed on a Sunday afternoon all the locos are at rest and out of steam, in a Victorian world of fizzing gas lamps, soot-encrusted beams and dripping water, and an atmosphere of warm oil, damp ashes and steam coal. In little more than 12 hours the scene will be transformed, as a dozen or more locos are lit up and steam raised in readiness for another working week. On cold winter mornings, the entire shed complex could become engulfed in a great cloud of steam and acrid part-combusted smoke, as shedmen and crews went about their work in the shadows. *RHM*

This is the adjacent repair shop on 2 February 1964, another S&WR location that remained in a time warp, with accommodation, services and much of the equipment little changed since the Victorian era, yet at a time when the cleaners could be found listening to the Beatles on their portable radios – if you knew where to find them. Almost to the end, the repair shop was in regular use for undertaking valve and piston exams, and any necessary light mechanical and boiler repairs. Pannier tank No 1650 may well have been the last locomotive to receive attention here. *RHM*

The west side of Lydney shed is seen here from what is locally known as 'Tinworks Hill', where the original tramroad route closely paralleled the lower section of Church Road. Tender locomotives diagrammed for the night-time Stoke Gifford working were often banished during the day to this siding alongside the shed, which only served to access the repair shop. On this occasion, in the late 1950s, the usual '43XX' Class 2-6-0 on the left is accompanied by '2251' Class 0-6-0 No 2291, another type that often undertook the Stoke Gifford turn, or was drafted in to work trainloads of Whitecliff ballast to other destinations on the Western Region. *RHM collection*

This is the rear of the shed, viewed past two withdrawn pannier tanks, Nos 8729 and 1626, on 10 March 1963. From left to right, the complex comprises the three-road running shed, the single-road repair shop and, beyond the water tanks, the two further bays then in use as stores by the civil engineer. The stationery boiler, in its corrugated iron shed, was fired up every week to enable boiler washouts to be conducted within the running shed. Beyond the mineral wagon, the white-painted building across Church Road formerly housed the Tinplate Works offices. *RHM*

Opposite top: **Dumped on the former engineer's siding at the rear of the shed some time in 1958 is BR Standard Class 4 4-6-0 No 75004, which had disgraced itself by failing at Lydney while hauling a Cardiff-Gloucester passenger train. The mangled remains of its right-hand valve gear – the cause of its failure – are clearly evident in this view. Sister locomotive No 75009, from Gloucester's ex-LMR Barnwood depot, was subsequently outstationed at Lydney for approximately two weeks in 1960. Being fitted with a tender cab, to facilitate tender-first running, it may well have been the intended successor to the spartan ex-GWR '43XX' Class 2-6-0s then diagrammed to work the nightly Lydney-Stoke Gifford goods.** *RHM*

Opposite: **From an allocation of 15 locomotives in 1960 to complete closure by March 1964, the run-down of Lydney loco depot was quite remarkable, reflecting the then rapid decline in the local coal industry and the loss of the Severn Bridge route, followed by a deliberate and systematic run-down of all local railway services, brought about by the Beeching Plan. This is the interior of Lydney shed on Friday 28 February 1964, with one of the last locomotives to work off shed, ex-GWR pannier tank No 4624. Following closure, all the shed buildings remained intact for more than two years, until, following the end of steam in 1965, there was no longer any need to retain the water tanks and other services. The site was cleared by June 1966 and has since been leased out to a succession of road hauliers.** *RHM*

Above: **On the last weekday of operations, Lydney driver Vic Rees signs on for duty at the shed office, with timekeeper Jim Darters also on his last shift before retirement.** *A. K. Pope, Coleford Railway Museum Collection*

10
Lydney Tinplate Works

Situated directly opposite the locomotive depot, on the west side of Church Road, was Lydney Tinplate Works, formerly owned by Richard Thomas & Baldwin and, from 1947, by the Steel Company of Wales. During the Second World War the works had been requisitioned by the Admiralty and utilised as a munitions store. However, following the cessation of hostilities, tinplate production resumed in September 1946, the works subsequently being modernised with new electrically powered rolling mills in 1956, only to face complete closure in November of the following year. In its heyday the works was a major employer in the town, and even into the early 1950s still had 450 workers on its payroll. The manufacturing process also generated considerable freight traffic for the railway, with inward movements, mostly from South Wales, of coal, steel bars and tin ingots, together with chemicals to aid the tinplating process, including sulphuric acid and palm oil. The tinplated steel produced at Lydney was of a high quality, and was dispatched in covered vans to many markets both home and abroad, Australia being one of the principal destinations. Among many British customers was Tate & Lyle, whose once familiar 'Golden Syrup' tins were made from Lydney tinplate.

This 1950s aerial view looking southwards down Church Road shows the works' proximity to the S&W railway yards (on the left), with the GWR main line also visible at the top of the picture. After closure, many of the buildings were demolished or adapted into workshops by the subsequent occupants, The Watts Group. *DFR Museum Trust collection*

Right: A clip from a 1939 photograph clearly illustrates the two sidings into the Tinworks diverging beneath the pair of '2021' Class pannier tanks within the loco shed yard, as well as the gated level crossing over Church Road and the Tinworks complex beyond.
V. R. Webster

Centre: The first locomotive to work at the tinplate works was this Ruston & Hornsby 0-4-0 diesel-mechanical shunter, No 221639, which was acquired new by the Admiralty in 1943. Initially based at the nearby salvage depot, the loco was transferred to the Tinworks for the remaining years of the Second World War while the site was being utilised as a munitions store. The loco subsequently worked for 30 more years in industrial service before moving to the Colne Valley Railway at Castle Hedingham, Essex, in 1978. *Ms S. Halls*

Below: This is the eastern end of the works, most of which dated from the late Victorian era, as viewed from Church Road level crossing shortly before closure in 1957, showing the sidings diverging to serve each side of the complex. To the left, by the signal, is the weighbridge and timekeeper's office, while beyond is the 'black pickling' shed, where newly rolled steel sheet was de-scaled in weak sulphuric acid. Next, right of centre, is the hot rolling mill, and finally, on the extreme right, the furnaces where newly cut steel bars were charged until they were red-hot and ready for feeding into the rolls. *Dean Heritage Museum Trust*

The sidings to the north side of the works were primarily used to receive wagons delivering coal to fire the furnaces and mill engines, and loads of steel bars (known as 'tin bars') for rolling into thin sheet metal for tinplating. It was on these sidings that the works' shunting locomotive and steam crane normally operated. In this view, set against a typical backdrop of coal wagons and stacks of 'tin bars', is the resident post-war shunter, *Peter Pan*, an 0-4-0 saddle tank built by Hudswell Clarke back in 1909, which had come to Lydney in 1946 from Morris Motors at Coventry.
DFR Museum Trust collection

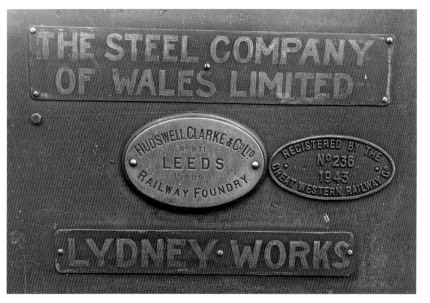

To enable *Peter Pan* to transfer between the two fans of sidings that served the works, it was necessary to venture over the level crossing onto tracks maintained by the GWR and LMS, and, after January 1948, by BR. Here is a close-up view of the loco's cabside showing the GWR registration plate authorising it to do so, together with one of the original 1909 worksplates.
A. A. Delicata

In 1953 *Peter Pan* was replaced by another 0-4-0 saddle tank, an Andrew Barclay product from Scotland, but which arrived from Carmarthenshire with a very Welsh name, *Glantawe*. After a respectable interval, AB 1180 was duly renamed *Lydney*, and remained in service, together with the steam crane, until the works closed in November 1957. Here the locomotive is undertaking light shunting duties outside the office building adjacent to Church Road. One of the Tinworks' level crossing gates is just visible beyond the front of the locomotive. *A. Neale collection*

Here is a rather ungainly looking *Lydney*, once again standing outside the Tinworks offices with its outsize partner, which, not surprisingly, was officially barred from running on BR metals – though it nevertheless did so from time to time. The steam crane was also utilised to undertake light shunting duties within the works when required. *C. Trigg*

Moving now to the south side of the works, this pre-war view shows the steeply graded sidings with stacks of empty boxes for tinplate opposite the railway vans and, on the left, drums of chemicals to aid the tinning process. Nowhere evident are any tin ingots, for, being of great value, they were all individually stamped upon arrival and secured under lock and key until required in the tin house. The south sidings were usually shunted by the S&W pilot, and retired locomen still recall the heavy loads that had to be dragged up this incline to the Church Road level crossing. During the post-war years many Italians and Eastern Europeans were brought in to ease the labour shortage at the works. Hostel accommodation was provided in prefabricated buildings erected within the foreground area (and visible in the aerial view on page 92), while the former manager's house on the right was adapted to provide communal facilities. *Dean Heritage Museum Trust*

Two of the principal ranges of workshops on the south side of the complex are seen here when in a state of semi-dereliction some ten years after closure. The building on the left with the ridge ventilator had housed the assorting and dispatch department, and the centre block had been the blacksmiths' shop, while the section featuring the square chimney flues had been the tin house. All have since been demolished. *S. V. Blencowe*

11
Lydney Engine Shed Junction to Lydney Town

Returning to the S&W system, we have now reached Engine Shed Junction (8m 28ch), with its replacement 26-lever box installed by the Midland Railway in 1918. Despite its modest size, this box was effectively the hub of the S&W system, controlling all traffic to and from the Forest, including the 'Third Line' and the weighbridge loop, as well as the routes to Severn Bridge, Lydney Yard, Lydney Docks, and access to the locomotive shed and the Tinworks. Until about 1960 it was open for up to 16 hours a day, six days a week, only closing on Sundays when there were no booked services. This is the view northwards in March 1964 with the S&W pilot about to set back onto a recently arrived up goods and mineral train. Beyond the loco are the connections between the S&W main line and the yard, then still confusingly titled 'Tinworks Junction', and, beyond the stop block, Engine Shed Ground Frame, which enabled locos to enter or leave the shed via the yard at times when the signal box was closed. *RHM*

Seen from a similar viewpoint on 14 April 1961, auto-fitted ex-GWR pannier tank No 6415 has the empty stock for the unadvertised 3.30pm Lydney Junction-Sharpness service, which, on each schoolday between October 1960 and July 1962, conveyed around 50 pupils from Lydney Grammar School back to their homes via Gloucester, a journey of nearly 40 miles. Until they were transferred to Rednock Grammar School at Dursley, LGS pupils from Sharpness and Berkeley were obliged to use three separate advertised BR services each morning (Sharpness-Berkeley Road, Berkeley Road-Gloucester Eastgate, and Gloucester Central-Lydney Junction), together with a coach connection for the final mile to the school. *The late R. Dagley-Morris*

This is the view on 7 July 1962 looking back to Engine Shed Junction, where today the Lydney Bypass now crosses the railway on the level. Had it not been for the existence of the DFRPS, the S&W line would have been terminated just short of this point (at 8m 33ch) when the branch was officially closed by BR in 1980. Seen here against the backdrop of an imminent thunderstorm is No 1631, pulling out of the yard with a train of empty mineral wagons bound for Parkend Marsh Sidings via Coleford Junction. Meanwhile, on the up line the S&W pilot is engaged in delivering coal for the signalman's stove. Until 1960 the buildings on the right housed the West of England Wagon Works, accessed from the S&W via a bridge over the adjacent Pidcock's Canal. *RHM*

Thirty-five years later, this is the point where the DFR meets the late 20th century, not so much head-on as at 90 degrees. With the half-barriers down and warning lights flashing, No 5541 heads an up 'Santa Special' over the Bypass crossing towards Lydney Junction in December 1997. The DFR's long-delayed extension, first to Lakeside Halt and later to Lydney Junction, ultimately worked to its advantage, since the Government's one-time aversion to such operations crossing trunk roads eased markedly during the intervening years. *RHM*

With effect from Monday 3 January 1966 all remaining BR freight services on the S&W lines were handed over to diesel traction. After an initial trip to Lydney Town earlier that morning, Swindon-built diesel-hydraulic 0-6-0 No D9522 heads north past Lydney churchyard with a healthy load of domestic coal for the local merchants. Just one trial run had previously been made over the line by another member of this class, No D9502, some four weeks earlier, on 3 December. Beyond the locomotive is the S&WR-built 'Churchfield House', which until early BR days was the residence of the Lydney Town station master. *RHM*

In a similar view dating from August 1999, ex-MR 0-6-0 tank No 41708 approaches with a Lydney to Norchard passenger service. The platform here, opened by the DFR on 17 August 1991, served as the railway's southern terminus, initially under the name of Lakeside Halt, and later as St Mary's Halt, until the extension to Lydney Junction S&W station opened on 2 June 1995. Visiting 'half cab' No 41708 is the last survivor of a long-lived class, first seen at Lydney as long ago as 1895, in the days before GWR motive power became the norm on the S&W west of the Severn. *RHM*

At a point directly opposite St Mary's Halt the railway crosses Pidcock's Canal, built in about 1790, at an acute angle as it pursues its course from Middle Forge, near Norchard, to Lower Forge, latterly the site of Lydney Tinplate Works. Long before the end of iron-making in the Lyd valley back in the 1890s, the canal had ceased to carry any commercial traffic, though it has since continued to provide a valuable resource as a water feeder to local industries. In 1956 the masonry-lined tunnel beneath the railway was opened up and replaced by two concrete culverts terminating in two extremely austere concrete headwalls. This is a late-1960s view from the canal towpath looking south-west towards St Mary's Halt and the now Grade 2 listed footbridge, which formerly spanned four tracks at this point. The DFR Museum Trust is still seeking any pre-1956 photos of the old tunnel portals. *S. V. Blencowe*

Weekend track renewals are in progress at a point opposite Bathurst Park between Engine Shed Junction and Lydney Town on 17 January 1961. In this view, looking north, ex-GWR pannier tank No 3721 is standing on the 'Third' or 'Mineral' line, used by up goods and mineral trains from the Forest en route to the Weighbridge Loop, the Yard or the Docks. The centre track, occupied by the crane, is the down main, used by all Forest-bound services, and that on the right, the up main, was used principally by passenger services to Berkeley Road. Up to the late 1950s the value of the 'Third' line became readily apparent every weekday afternoon, as up to three or four trains queued head-to-tail awaiting access to Lydney Yard. *The late R. Dagley-Morris*

12
Lydney Town station

Located in the very heart of Lydney, Town station (8m 73ch) appeared in its later days to be a somewhat unremarkable establishment, with two platforms, 'the usual offices', and an adjacent goods yard served by three sidings. However, a more critical look reveals a rather more interesting picture since, in its former S&WR days, the site had also housed certain key facilities essential for the day-to-day operation of an independent railway, some of which lasted well into BR days. Although taken in the mid-1950s, this aerial view looking south reveals an infrastructure little changed since late-Victorian times.

Taking a brief clockwise tour around the site, starting from the Hill Street level crossing of the A48, the following buildings and features can be clearly identified. On the up (nearest) platform, adjacent to the auto-train, are the original timber-framed station buildings dating from the commencement of passenger services in 1875, then, over the rear wall, the former Lydney Foundry, rebuilt in 1858 and originally specialising in the manufacture of railway track components. For many years after 1892 this S&W-owned site was leased to a brewery company for use as a rail-served beer store, before finally ending its days as a distribution depot for Corona soft drinks.

Crossing now to the west side of the tracks, at the south (left-hand) end of the site are the cattle pen and end-loading dock, accessed from Bathurst Park Road. The adjacent one-time rail-served building, with its attached water tank, was apparently built to house the S&WR General Manager's Inspection Saloon, although it was later used as a stable and blacksmith's shop. Within the goods yard, unusually enclosed by high masonry walls, are further engineer's stores and workshops abutting the boundary wall, together with a two-storey builders' merchant's warehouse, and the standard Gloucester Wagon Co timber-framed goods shed, which incorporated an internal hand crane.

Finally, on the down platform stands the masonry base of the original signal box, adapted into a staff mess room and offices, then the standard GWR-design red-brick station building, added in 1897, the contemporary replacement 26-lever GWR signal box, with wheel-operated gates, and the footbridge added in 1904 in response to pressure from the local council. Just visible on the right, opposite the goods yard, is 'Severn House', former residence of the S&WR General Manager, and next door, directly adjoining the level crossing, his coachman's cottage. *DFR Museum Trust collection*

Seen here from the south end of the down platform in June 1964 are two ex-GWR '57XX' Class pannier tanks returning to Lydney Junction with the daily goods and mineral working from Coleford. They are being diverted onto the 'Third' line on the right to enable them to take their train directly into Lydney Yard. The mature trees on the right mark the beginning of Bathurst Park, which bounds the railway for more than a quarter of a mile to a point just short of the 'iron bridge'. *RHM*

A similar view some 27 years later illustrates the state into which the railway had deteriorated prior to its purchase by the DFR in 1985. This was then a rare working over the southern end of the DFR's line to collect some new items of rolling stock from Lydney Yard. The locomotive in action here is Rolls Royce Sentinel No 10165, one of two 0-4-0 diesel-hydraulic shunters that came from Panteg steelworks, near Cwmbran, in 1989. Note the second-hand concrete sleepers offloaded ready to replace life-expired timbers beneath the adjacent running line. *RHM*

This is the approach to the Town station from the south on 27 May 1966, with BR diesel-hydraulic 0-6-0 No D9501 crossing over to the 'Third' line with a train of empty coal wagons. At this time the goods yard was still intact and in daily use for domestic coal traffic, although the running lines had been rationalised in February 1965. The buildings visible beyond the goods yard, fronting onto Hill Street, are the former S&WR company offices (left) and the S&WR General Manager's house (right). The offices were not sold out of railway use until 1934, and for many years since have provided accommodation for the Lydney branch of the British Legion. *RHM*

Returning to more halcyon days, this is the southward prospect from the footbridge on 3 June 1957, with ex-GWR 0-4-2 tank No 1430 propelling its two auto-trailers over the crossover before drawing back into the up platform to form the next southbound departure. The angle of the shadows and the sizeable gathering of passengers, many with bags and suitcases, indicates that this will be the 10.50am to Berkeley Road, where a booked 4-minute connection could be made with a semi-fast to Bristol Temple Meads, then still the gateway to a host of West Country holiday destinations. *A. Jarvis*

This view, dating from August 1947, once again features auto-fitted pannier tank No 2080 and its two GWR auto-trailers standing in the up platform awaiting departure. Given that this image dates from the time of post-war coal shortages, the S&WJR board on the platform interestingly gives notice of cancellation of the 4.25pm weekday departure to Berkeley Road for the six weeks of the school holidays between late July and early September: This was the service that on each schoolday normally conveyed 50 or so Lydney Grammar School pupils back to their homes east of the Severn. *W. A. Camwell, courtesy of Stephenson Locomotive Society*

Another photograph and another age: this is the same up platform on 10 October 1970, by now stripped of all its buildings, fittings, and even its stone edging slabs. The view is from the decommissioned signal box, which is soon to be demolished, while the former Lydney Foundry, here providing the backdrop, will also disappear within a matter of months. On the positive side, the approaching Gloucester RC&W-built 'Cross Country' DMU is the first of many special trains to be chartered by the DFRPS. This train, the 'Severnside Venturer', is about to call at Lydney Town to provide the first opportunity for DFR Society members and others to entrain for a round trip over the S&W line to Parkend. *RHM*

Next are two contrasting views looking northwards from the station, yet with less than a decade between them. The first, from June 1964, shows a mid-afternoon scene that had changed little over the preceding 50 years. Centre stage are two Gloucester-based pannier tanks, Nos 3745 and 4624, heading through with the returning Coleford to Lydney freight. The fireman of the second locomotive is about to surrender the single-line tablet to the waiting signalman. *RHM*

The date is now 17 June 1972, the signal box has closed, and weeds and undergrowth are taking over. Since May 1971 the daily trip working to Parkend has no longer come from Gloucester, but instead from Severn Tunnel Junction. Traffic from the railhead at Parkend is now confined to track ballast delivered by road from Whitecliff Quarry, and to wagon loads of opencast-mined coal bound for the CEGB's power stations. On this occasion STJ has unusually diagrammed a Class 31 Brush diesel-electric, No 5828, which has recently been transferred from the Eastern Region and is still carrying its BR green livery. Also noteworthy is that the old GWR 'Herring' ballast hoppers, so long a feature of the Whitecliff workings, have been replaced by higher-capacity BR-built 'Dogfish' hoppers, a type subsequently preserved on the DFR. *S. V. Blencowe*

This road-user's view of Lydney Town on a dank and drizzly morning in April 1965 is at a time when the old A48 trunk road was still one of the major links between England and South Wales (the opening of the First Severn Crossing was still another 16 months away). Everything comes to a standstill as the bulky profile of a GWR 'large Prairie' tank locomotive heads southwards over the crossing with a train of empty ballast wagons from Tintern Quarry. The reason for this one-off visitation will become clear in the next volume. To the right is Lydney Town signal box, and to the left the mean BR-owned cottage that was originally home to the S&WR General Manager's coachman. *RHM*

This was the northward prospect once afforded from the footbridge until its demise in 1962. Beyond the level crossing, the running line immediately becomes single for the ensuing 1¾ miles to Tufts Junction. Of note is the catch point installed during the 1950s on the down line to prevent any runaways from reaching the level crossing, albeit to the detriment of any occupants in the coachman's cottage! Also unusual is the positioning of both running line signals outside the railway fence. On the right are sidings serving the Lydney & Chepstow Trading Co, builders' merchants, and T. S. Thomas & Sons, coal merchants, all occupying a wide shelf cut into the hillside after the railway was realigned onto a more direct course than its predecessor, the tramroad. No regular passenger services ran north of Lydney Town after 6 July 1929, though excursion trains continued to serve some S&W line stations until 1961. *RHM*

Following the closure of all railway facilities at Lydney Town during the 1960s, every BR structure was quickly demolished, to be replaced during the following decade by a shopping complex on the former foundry site, and by a new fire station and a row of houses in what had been the goods yard. This is the brave new world of Lydney Town looking south in July 1988 with the widened A48 crossing now protected by tubular steel gates and every trace of the old S&W infrastructure, except for one single track, completely swept away. *Wilbert* heads northward with a DFR works train. *RHM*

Thanks to the co-operation of one of the new landowners, the DFR was subsequently able to squeeze in a new single-platform station on the east side of the running line. Complete with its replica of the original station building, and funded in part by a Rural Development Grant, this facility was opened to the public on 22 April 2001. Heading southward barely a month later, on 18 May, is EWS-owned Class 37 diesel-electric No 37308, undertaking a trial run with empty coaching stock in preparation for the diesel gala that was to take place over the ensuing weekend. *RHM*

13
Lydney Town to Norchard

Rounding the first curve just north of Lydney Town station, the landscape suddenly changes as the hills close in, the gradient stiffens and the Forest looms ahead. On the first sweeping curve, seen here, the S&W formation appears to be of sufficient width for at least six tracks, yet for the past 130 years it has carried only one. The reason for this anomaly is that the railway's predecessor, the tramroad, was economically built to hug the contours with minimal earthworks, often resulting in tight curves that its successor was unable to follow, requiring new formations to ease the alignment. Also, during the S&WR's transition period from tramroad to railway both systems operated side-by-side for many miles, requiring retention of a double-track formation. In this April 1970 view up the valley, a North British-built Class 22 diesel-hydraulic is approaching Lydney with the Gloucester breakdown train's packing van and mess coach after attending to a derailment at Parkend. Until its demise in the 1890s the Middle Forge complex was located next to the River Lyd just beyond the cultivated field. *RHM*

The same section of line just over 21 years later presents a very different aspect with dense foliage and 40-foot-high trees crowding in on both sides of the line. Over recent years the DFR has cleared back most of the lineside vegetation to 'steam age' standards. In this August 1991 view, visiting GWR 4-4-0 No 3440 *City of Truro* is heading a southbound service on the approach to Lydney Town. *RHM*

After barely a quarter mile, the S&W is crossed by a narrow lane that once provided the only access to the Middle Forge ironworks. At this location, now designated 'Middle Forge Junction' by the DFR, there was also, between 1906 and 1948, a ground frame controlling the southern outlet from Norchard Colliery, from which loaded wagons were collected after passing through the screens. The MR 'half cab' 0-6-0 tank, this time in the guise of a former Gloucester Barnwood depot locomotive, is seen heading southwards over the old crossing in August 1994. *RHM*

In 1973, at a time when BR still seemed intent upon retaining the S&W line to Parkend, the DFRPS identified the then disused sites of Norchard Power Station, Norchard Colliery, and the half-mile long formation of the former outlet siding, as being ideal for redevelopment into a steam centre. Negotiations were successfully progressed with the landowners – the CEGB and Bathurst Park Estates – such that the Society was able to begin site clearance works later that year. Reconnection of the Norchard siding to the former S&W line was not achieved, however, until 1986, after BR had completed its sale to the DFR. After gradually extending a push-pull service to a point just short of Lydney Town level crossing, the DFR was eventually able to expand its operations over the A48 to Lakeside Halt, at a point just short of the proposed Lydney Bypass. On 8 September 1991 *City of Truro* is heading north past Middle Forge with one of the returning special trains to officially celebrate that achievement. *RHM*

The DFR DMU Group's two-car Class 108 unit reverses at Middle Forge prior to undertaking a route-learning trip along the branch in March 2000. Since its entry into DFR service in 1993, the unit, soon to be lengthened into a three-car formation, has proved a valuable asset to the railway. Even after BR's introduction of 'Sprinter' trains on the Gloucester-Cardiff route in the mid-1980s, these Derby-built units, dating back to 1958, continued to work some of the main-line services calling at Lydney station until 1991. *RHM*

As seen earlier on page 59, the Monmouthshire Railway Society's 'Gwaun Cae Gurwen Growler' of Saturday 23 April 1994 became the first main-line railtour to travel over the DFR-owned line to Norchard Low Level. Here seen approaching Middle Forge, the eight-coach train is made up of early BR Mark II stock 'topped and tailed' by two Class 37 diesel-electric locos, Nos 37402 and 37258. *RHM*

Middle Forge was the setting for an unplanned sequel to the diesel gala held on the railway over the weekend of 19/20 May 2001. During their brief stay on the DFR, Railtrack tickets authorising the main-line operation for three of the EWS 'heritage' diesel locomotives on show expired, with the result that they became stranded on the DFR. Eight days later, with the bureaucrats appeased, the locos are seen being re-marshalled for onward movement to Lydney Junction, from where they were to be collected by EWS. Note that the track layout has changed once again, with the junction now controlled by a ground frame released by the single line token. *RHM*

Heading north from Middle Forge, the two tracks run parallel for approximately 250 yards before the right-hand formation to Norchard Low Level drops steeply down onto a narrow ledge between the Parkend line embankment and the River Lyd. Considerable works have been necessary to regrade and realign this former colliery line to bring it up to passenger-carrying standards. This northward view clearly depicts the left-hand line to Parkend steadily climbing at 1 in 170, and the colliery line falling sharply away towards the bottom of the valley. Though still barely a mile from Lydney Town, the railway is already becoming totally dominated by the hills and the Forest. Against this timeless backdrop the DFDA's preserved BR SR electro-diesel No E6001 heads southwards with empty coaching stock on 9 May 2009. *RHM*

Moving a few hundred yards closer to Norchard, another pair of 'before' and 'after' images of the DFR illustrate once again the transformation that has been wrought in recent years. On the high-level line to Parkend, this April 1971 view features the daily 'tripper' in charge of a scruffy North British Class 22 diesel-hydraulic, No D6354, then barely 10 years old, but already working out its last month of service with BR. Beyond the loco and its train, and concealed beneath 20-plus years of prolific undergrowth, lies the trackbed of the low-level exit siding from Norchard Colliery. *RHM*

A similar view, albeit through a telephoto lens, taken in May 2009, shows the low-level route cleared and the track relaid and signalled to passenger-carrying standards. GWR pannier tank No 9681 is heading southwards on yet another 'branch line experience' trip with the DFR's capacious SR 'Queen Mary' brake-van in tow. *RHM*

Now on the final approach to Norchard, here are two further views from the archives of past operations. On the former colliery line, Hunslet 0-6-0 saddle tank No 3806 approaches the 5mph speed-restricted section adjoining the River Lyd. At the time of this April 1989 view the DFR was only operating a shuttle service to a point just north of Lydney Town level crossing. Push-pull operation was achieved by attaching a goods brake-van fitted with an audio warning device and an additional brake-setter for operation by the guard. Prior to its purchase for preservation in 1972, No 3806 had been one of a small fleet of well-maintained NCB shunters based at Cannock Colliery in Staffordshire. *RHM*

Proceeding even more cautiously through recently cleared undergrowth on the high-level S&W line is former Port of Bristol Authority's No 39, a Rolls Royce Sentinel diesel-hydraulic 0-6-0 shunter that had previously worked at Avonmouth Docks. Attached is the GW150 travelling exhibition train that, during its intensive tour of the UK during the summer of 1985, came to Norchard High Level for just two days, 17 and 18 August, before moving on once more. At the time the DFR had recently purchased the branch from BR and was thus able to utilise its own motive power to transfer this heavy eight-coach train from and to Lydney Junction. *D. Snook*

14
Norchard

As with many industrial locations in the Forest of Dean, the former Norchard Colliery site now occupied by the Dean Forest Railway has a long and complex history. The site first became rail-connected in 1879 when a siding, known as Kidnalls Siding, was laid from the S&WR, curving through the site to bridge the River Lyd before terminating in tramroad transfer sidings on the eastern side of what is now Forest Road.

The development of a major colliery complex on the site did not commence until about 1900, but was quickly followed by the erection of screens to grade and load the coal into railway wagons, and by the provision of the 'low-level' exit siding. All railway wagon movements on the site were achieved by gravity, hence there was never any requirement for a shunting locomotive, or even a horse. In 1923 the West Gloucestershire Power Company built its generating station on an adjacent site between the River Lyd and Forest Road, and installed an overhead conveyor to deliver coal directly from the screens to storage hoppers located directly above the boiler house. Since the coal mined at Norchard burned so fiercely, it always had to be blended with supplies from other local collieries.

In 1938 a new pit-head and screens, called New Norchard Colliery, was established some 1½ miles to the north, at Pillowell, to provide a more cost-effective means of accessing the remaining coal measures. Output from the old Norchard Colliery therefore ceased in 1938, though coal deliveries by rail for the power station were still maintained from New Norchard and other Forest pits. In 1960 the remaining siding connection was removed, leaving the power station solely dependent upon road deliveries for the remaining years of its operational life.

In its quest for an operating base and visitor centre, the then recently formed Dean Forest Railway Preservation Society soon identified the Norchard Colliery site as being potentially ideal for its needs, especially with the adjacent power station site able to provide the all-important car-parking facility for visitors. Since closure of the colliery and the power station, all remaining structures had been demolished, and ownership of the colliery site had reverted to the Bathurst Park Estate. Following initial enquiries by the society in 1973, negotiations to acquire both sites, together with the former outlet siding, proved fruitful, such that access became possible later that year, enabling the mammoth task of redevelopment to begin.

Good working relations with the Army Apprentices School at Beachley led to the former colliery site being cleared and regraded by its engineers within a matter of weeks during 1974, while DFRPS volunteers soon set about establishing the necessary trackwork and infrastructure. By January 1978 development of the site was sufficiently advanced to enable the society to transfer its locomotives and rolling stock from Parkend. Thanks to the co-operation of the BR Area Manager, this was achieved by moving all operational stock by rail in one special BR-hauled train to the location of the former siding connection into Norchard Colliery, where a temporary track slew enabled all stock to be transferred to the new site.

Over the ensuing 30-plus years, the DFR has constructed station platforms on both the high- and low-level lines, together with a restoration shed and storage sidings, all controlled from an operational signal box. The site also serves as the principal visitor centre for the railway, with its booking office, buffet, shop and museum. Future plans include improved passenger facilities, and provision of more covered accommodation for the railway's collection of historic locomotives and rolling stock. One imminent project is the development of an on-site hydro-electric generating plant, which should meet most of the DFR's power requirements at Norchard. This unique opportunity arises as a consequence of the old Norchard drift now being the lowest outlet point from many inter-connected underground Forest mine workings, most of which, when operational, required constant pumping to prevent them from flooding. Since the last deep mine closed in 1965, no pumping has been carried out, with the result that between 10,000 and 14,000 gallons of water now flow out of the workings every minute, year on year, with the capability of providing an assured and ongoing source of power.

In the early 1970s one had to be both a visionary and an optimist to see the potential of the Norchard Colliery site, for this is the way it was before any development work took place. The prospect here is looking northward from a point just below the site of the present signal box, as recorded in the summer of 1973. To the left, the route of the S&W line is hidden by trees and undergrowth, while on the right the old waste tip is developing a healthy covering of shrubs and silver birch. *S. V. Blencowe*

Another northward view, dating from April 1961, shows some of the derelict colliery buildings still extant at that time. In the left foreground is the base of the conveyor to the power station, and beyond is the detached cottage which pre-dated the colliery, yet amazingly remained occupied throughout all its years of operation, and indeed for another 30 years or so afterwards. At the far end of the site is the brick-built chimney stack, and beneath it the ruins of the boiler house that had once powered the steam-driven water pumps and turbine generators – for the mine had been equipped with electricity since its earliest days. On the right are the former blacksmiths' shop and the overgrown ruins of the haulage house. There was no vertical mine shaft here, the entrances comprising two 'levels' driven into the hillside directly beneath the S&WR opposite the north end of the DFR's low-level platform. *The late R. Dagley-Morris*

Returning to the S&W line, this is the tiny MR cabin that, until 1960, contained the two-lever ground frame giving access to Norchard Colliery Sidings (9m 52ch). The point connection here, which could only be unlocked by the electric train tablet, formed the northern entrance to a loop line that, since 1948, had been cut back to form a headshunt for the one siding latterly retained into the colliery site. Most of the coal delivered here by rail for the power station travelled less than 2 miles from New Norchard Colliery at Pillowell. *L. E. Copeland, Wild Swan Publications Ltd*

This is the original north-end point connection, as recorded in March 1948. The photographer is standing in the '4 foot' of the S&W main line, looking north, with the former loop line to Middle Forge extending back in the right foreground, and the colliery line – then still known as Kidnalls Siding – curving and dropping away to the right. The coal off-loading point onto the conveyor to the power station is just out of sight behind the silver birch trees. Standing sentinel is the fixed Up Distant signal for Lydney Town, a joint-line hybrid, comprising a GWR timber post and finial fitted with a later LMS upper-quadrant arm. *L. E. Copeland, Wild Swan Publications Ltd*

Here, heading past Norchard with a full payload on Sunday 23 September 1973, is one of several such special excursions that were chartered by the DFRPS in the early 1970s to bring visitors to its open days at Parkend. This train had run from Bristol, via Gloucester, to Parkend, from where it then operated several shuttle services to and from a point just north of Lydney Town, before returning to Bristol. These 'Oakleaf Flyers', usually comprising BR Class 117 (as here) or 119 three-car DMUs, proved both popular and remunerative, and gave many visitors an early opportunity to sample a return trip over the branch at a very affordable walk-on fare. Just visible through the luxuriant foliage are the ruins of Alice Lee's cottage, the society's recently delivered GWR van body, and a new hoarding bravely proclaiming 'NORCHARD – DFRPS NEW SITE'. *RHM*

The site of the former northern connection into Norchard Colliery as viewed from the brake-van of the very last BR freight train to run from Parkend, comprising opencast-mined coal destined for the power stations at Uskmouth and Portishead. The date is Friday 7 May 1976. The locomotive is Class 37 diesel-electric No 37270, which, in later life as No 37409 *Loch Awe*, became one of a select band of Scottish Region locomotives allocated to work the West Highland line. It still survives in the Direct Rail Services fleet based at Carlisle. *F. C. Scoon*

Norchard's renaissance really began from the day the society's modest collection of locos and rolling stock arrived by rail from Parkend on the dark and drizzly morning of 16 January 1978. Here is the special BR train, headed by one of the last Class 25 diesel-electrics to visit the S&W line – No 25036 – cautiously approaching from Parkend, with restored GWR 'Prairie' tank No 5541 clearly in 'light steam only for lubrication purposes'. On the right, the original steeply graded connection down to the colliery site has been relaid by the DFRPS ready to receive the new arrivals. *F. C. Scoon*

After DFRPS volunteers had slewed the track under the supervision of the BR Area Manager, the society's Hunslet 0-4-0 diesel No 2145 was employed to haul the stock over the temporary connection and into the Society's new home. Like all other such fixed signals on the branch, Lydney Town's Up Distant, shown here, was retained after all operating signals on the branch had been decommissioned in October 1967. *P. Skinner, DFR Museum Trust collection*

Passenger train operations commenced at Norchard in March 1978, initially with Peckett 0-4-0 saddle tank No 2147 *Uskmouth 1* and ex-GWR auto-trailer No 167 shuttling to and fro over approximately 150 yards of the former colliery connection from the S&W line. *DFR Museum Trust collection*

Station facilities were likewise somewhat basic. The top of Gloucester Mileage Yard signal box (left) served as staff accommodation, while the original S&WR station building from Drybrook Road, which for the previous 20 years had served as an office in a Steam Mills timber yard, provided but spartan accommodation for visitors. Also just visible beyond is the DFR's first catering facility – a former BR restaurant car stabled in the bay platform. All these facilities were swept away in 1995, though both the signal box and the platform sections were reused. *DFR Museum Trust collection*

As the Norchard site was progressively developed through the 1980s, the now familiar layout and facilities became established, the last major piece of the jigsaw being the high-level platform, on the Parkend line, which opened in 2004. The extent of the DFR's achievements during those years can most effectively be illustrated by some further 'before' and 'after' images. This April 1968 scene, looking south, features the 1923-built conveyor by which coal was originally fed direct from the colliery screens into storage bunkers above the power station boiler furnaces, and later from rail deliveries off-loaded into a collection hopper at its base. The conveyor, which had spanned the former outlet sidings from the screens, the waste tip and the River Lyd, was demolished during the latter months of 1968, although its substantial concrete base remained in situ until the arrival of the DFR. To the right is the cottage that had been tenanted until but a few months earlier. For many years this property was known as 'Alice Lee's cottage' after a former occupant. *RHM*

Fast forward to a completely transformed scene in 2001, during the diesel gala held on Saturday 19 May. Visiting preserved Class 37 diesel-electric No 37029 is approaching Norchard Low Level with a passenger working from Lydney Junction, which will return behind GWR 'small Prairie' tank locomotive No 5541, seen here waiting on the run-round loop. *RHM*

A lunchtime break is taken during the Beachley Army Apprentices' exercise to clear and grade the former colliery site in July 1974. After some tropical summer weather, the whole area was turned into a most impressive black mud-bath, but at the end of just a few weeks' work, which saved the DFR many thousands of pounds, most of the site was cleared and levelled ready for the laying of drainage and track ballast. During the clearance stage, a number of old rails were unearthed, and also a short section of the colliery's 22 ½ -inch-gauge dram lines still set into a concrete base. This southward view, which shows the old masonry retaining wall opposite the former screens, is taken from a position now occupied by the southern end of the low-level platform. On the right is a GWR railway van body that initially provided the DFR's only accommodation on the site. *RHM*

During the site clearance works, much of the former waste tip was removed in order to level up the yard areas and create the additional space now occupied by the locomotive sidings and the restoration shed. Hence this view is from a point previously within the tip behind the retaining walls seen above. GWR 0-4-2 tank loco No 1450 is approaching the low-level platform with restored GWR auto-trailer No 178. Norchard's ex-GWR 13-lever signal box was originally recovered in the early 1970s from Gloucester where, as Mileage Yard Ground Frame, it had controlled the entrances to the Old Yard and Horton Road locomotive depot. The box was recommissioned at Norchard in August 1996. *RHM*

In the early days at Norchard, economy and ingenuity were essential in establishing basic facilities at minimal cost – and sometimes it showed. These are some of the original locomotive repair facilities, albeit backed up by stores and mess vans, which were still in use in 1988. The roof structure here is scaffold tubing clad with corrugated plastic sheeting, with a canvas-sheeted lean-to – all very Colonel Stephens, but well short of the old S&WR's standards, even during the company's leanest years. *P. Skelton*

By 1992, thanks in part to assistance from the Manpower Services Commission, the railway was able to construct this three-road restoration shed to provide levels of accommodation and working conditions more in line with 20th-century expectations. Even here, economy remained a watchword, for the steel roof trusses had previously been salvaged at minimal cost from a redundant industrial building in Newport. The ex-Barry scrapyard locomotive seen here undergoing restoration in July 2001 is privately owned ex-GWR 'small Prairie' tank No 5521. This locomotive later moved to the Flourmill Colliery workshops at Bream for completion, before embarking on a high-profile visit to Eastern Europe. During an eventful two-year tour, it acquitted itself well on main-line passenger services in Poland, and at one point even piloted the 'Orient Express'. A more modest debut on DFR duties followed in September 2009. *R. Jones*

Among the many locomotives that have visited Norchard in recent times have been two historic working replicas from the National Railway Museum at York. Seen first is the GWR broad gauge 4-2-2 *Iron Duke* of 1847, which, despite its girth, arrived by rail on a standard gauge well wagon, albeit with its chimney removed. Both the locomotive and its tender were displayed at Norchard during the visit of the GW150 exhibition train in August 1985.

The second picture shows the NRM's replica of Stephenson's *Rocket*, the locomotive that made history at the Liverpool & Manchester Railway's Rainhill Trials of 1830. The replica, built in 1980 for the Rainhill 150 event, was consigned to the Flourmill Colliery for overhaul in 1996, and is seen here in ex-works condition after movement to Norchard for running-in trials at Easter 1997. *Gloucestershire Media/A. Copley*

To round off this brief visit to Norchard is a further handful of images of the site since it has become established as the DFR's operating base. For nearly 20 years now this once obscure location has become widely recognised as a modest but unique steam centre where an ever-changing programme of events and exhibits continues to pull in the visitors year on year. Tucked away in the woods, and surrounded by the ruins and ghosts of former industries, Norchard has managed to perpetuate some of the quirkiness and charm of the old S&W Joint Railway in a setting that itself exudes something of both the history and mystery that still pervades this unique little corner of England.

On Sunday 8 September 1991, the sun is shining and the band is playing. The NRM's famous GWR 4-4-0 *City of Truro* and the DFR's *Wilbert* have just arrived at the new low-level platform with the official reopening train from Lydney Lakeside. *City of Truro's* brief visit to the railway brought record numbers of visitors to see the first steam locomotive in the world to exceed 100mph. *RHM*

On Saturday 23 April 1994 Norchard Low Level hosts its first main-line railtour, the Monmouthshire Railway Society's 'Gwaun Cae Gurwen Growler', seen earlier at Lydney Junction and Middle Forge. The leading locomotive, Class 37 diesel-electric No 37402 *Bont Y Bermo/Barmouth Bridge*, is one of many with Cambrian Coast connections that have visited the S&W line in recent times. *DFR Museum Trust collection*

This panoramic view of the Norchard site on 27 May 2001 was taken from the old waste tip and was achieved thanks to recent clearance of some of the prolific undergrowth that constantly threatens to overwhelm this section of the railway. Centre stage is GWR 'small Prairie' tank No 5541 arriving with a service from Lydney Junction, while on the high-level line the three stranded EWS diesel locos (see page 111) still await their new Railtrack 'tickets'. The buildings on the low-level platform comprise a GWR waiting shelter and an MR crossing-keeper's cabin, each reflecting the architectural styles of the two companies that formerly jointly managed the S&WR. *RHM*

Finally, a rare image of a BR passenger train – actually empty stock – heading past the site of Norchard Colliery on its way to Parkend to form a day excursion one hot summer's day in 1960. At its head, the hard-working locomotive is one of Lydney's stud of ex-GWR '57XX' Class pannier tanks, while the coaches are all modern BR Mk 1 vehicles, newly painted in the latest lined-out maroon livery. If authority, in its many forms, had won the day, sights such as this would have disappeared for all time from the Forest, and indeed from the rest of the UK, by the mid-1960s. Instead, 50 years on, the DFR is still able to assemble and run an almost identical train over this scenic route. *M. V. Rees, Coleford Railway Museum*

Norchard Power Station

Finally, we make a brief detour across the River Lyd to the site of what is now the DFR's car park but which, over the years between 1923 and 1968, accommodated the largest coal-fired power station in the county.

Opened in 1923 by the West Gloucestershire Power Company Ltd, Norchard Power Station provided supplies throughout the Forest of Dean and also, via submarine cables, to many parts of the county east of the Severn, including Stroud, Nailsworth, Dursley and Thornbury, while further transmission lines ran to Gloucester and Chepstow.

The main complex, which amazingly was constructed and commissioned within just six months, comprised three linked buildings, all steel-framed and clad in red brick. These were the boiler house, the turbine house and, at the front, facing Forest Road, the switch room. The site was chosen for its close proximity to abundant sources of coal, most of which, as we have already seen, was delivered by an overhead conveyor from Norchard Colliery, and to the presence of a consistently dependable water supply from the River Lyd. Both the boiler house and the turbine house were designed to accommodate further extensions, though only the latter was ever so altered. Power from the station was routed to an adjacent transformer station from where it was transmitted at 33,000kV on overhead lines supported by the company's distinctive steel pylons, many of which have survived into the 21st century.

With the decline of mining and heavy industry in the county, and the opening of new nuclear power stations at Berkeley and Oldbury in the 1960s, Norchard Power Station was initially reduced to winter-time operation only and finally to emergency reserve status, before facing closure in 1968, and demolition over the ensuing winter months of 1968-69.

The power station site is seen from the west side of the valley above the railway in 1964. The overhead conveyor from the colliery site is visible on the left, as are the corrugated iron claddings to the south elevations of the buildings, provided to readily accommodate any later extensions. To the right are the two later-built cooling towers, while between them the aerial ropeway for ash disposal can be seen crossing Forest Road and heading up the hillside to the tip. *DFR Museum Trust collection*

Where visitors to Norchard now park their cars in the vicinity of the old railway signal was, until 1968, the power station's turbine house, capable of generating up to 17,500kW from steam generated from three giant boilers in the adjacent boiler house. Steam was fed to these turbines at a pressure of 260psi, superheated to 650°F. Initially, all condensing water was drawn from and then returned to the River Lyd, but when another set of generators was

added in 1928, provision of the concrete cooling tower became necessary. The timber-framed tower was added in 1942 to ensure that there would always be sufficient water available to enable all the generators to run at full capacity. *DFR Museum Trust collection*

The Telfer aerial ropeway is seen from the east side of the valley in 1968, looking down onto the covered way over Forest Road to the point where the loaded ash skips were transferred from a narrow gauge tramway from the boiler house. The S&W line can just be glimpsed to the right of the cooling tower. *Dean Heritage Museum Trust collection*

Our last view of the S&W line in this volume, taken just above Norchard in February 1998, features the DFR's own ex-NCB Hunslet 0-6-0 tank loco No 3806 hard at work hauling one of the many trainloads of fresh track ballast that were imported by the DFR from the Peak District during 1998 and 1999 in order to upgrade the relaid track to Parkend. As each section of the line was restored, DFR services were extended in stages to Tufts Junction, Whitecroft, and finally Parkend, which was reached in December 2005. In the next volume the DFR's reopened line to Parkend will be featured, together with all the other long-closed sections of the Severn & Wye Railway system that once ran through the Forest to serve Coleford, Lydbrook and Cinderford. *B. J. Ashworth*

Bibliography

Barnett, Bob *Dean Forest Footplate Memories* (2007: Silver Link Publishing Ltd)

Conway-Jones, Hugh *The Gloucester & Sharpness Canal – an Illustrated History* (2003: Tempus Publishing Ltd)

Field, Dr Graham J. *A Look Back at Norchard* (1978: Author; reprinted 2009)

Hart, Cyril *The Industrial History of Dean* (1971: David & Charles (Publishers) Ltd)

Huxley, Ron *The Rise and Fall of the Severn Railway Bridge* (1984: Alan Sutton; reprinted 2008 by Amberley Publishing)

Mitchell, Vic and Smith, Keith *Branch Lines around Lydney* (2008: Middleton Press)

Paar, H. W. *The Severn & Wye Railway* (1963: David & Charles (Publishers) Ltd; reprinted 1973)

Parkhouse, Neil *A Glance Back at Lydney Docks* (2001: Black Dwarf Publications)

Pope, Ian, How, Bob and Karau, Paul *The Illustrated History of the Severn & Wye Railway*, Vol 1 (1983: Wild Swan Publications Ltd; reprinted 2003)

Smith, Peter *An Illustrated Historical Survey of the Forest of Dean Railways* (1983: Oxford Publishing Company)

Stretton, John *The Dean Forest Railway & ex-Severn & Wye Railway Lines*, Vols 1 & 2 (2002 & 2007: Past & Present Publishing Ltd)

Back numbers of the DFR Society's magazine covering many aspects of the railway's renaissance over the past four decades.

Abbreviations

The following abbreviations have been extensively used throughout the text and captions:

B&GR	Bristol & Gloucester Railway (1839-45)
BR	British Railways (1948-96)
BWB	British Waterways Board (post-1963)
DFDA	Dean Forest Diesel Association
DFR	Dean Forest Railway
DFRPS	Dean Forest Railway Preservation Society
EWS	English Welsh & Scottish Railways (post-1996)
GW/GWR	Great Western Railway (1835-1948)
LMS/LMSR	London Midland & Scottish Railway (1923-1948)
MR	Midland Railway (1844-1923)
S&W&SBR	Severn & Wye & Severn Bridge Railway (1879-94)
S&W/S&WR	Severn & Wye Railway & Canal Company (1810-79)
S&WJR	Severn & Wye Joint Railway (1894-1948)
SWR	South Wales Railway (1850-63)

Index of locations

Berkeley	20-21
Berkeley Loop Junction	16-17
Berkeley Road	9-16
South Junction	18
Lydney (GWR)	67-71, 81
Junction signal box	58-60
West signal box and flat crossing	70-71, 81, 82
Lydney (S&WR)	61-66, 85
Engine Shed Junction	97-99
Lakeside	99-100
Shed	86-91
Town station	101-107
Yard	61, 66, 81
Lydney Docks, Lower Docks branch and Tidal Basin	76-80
Pine End works	74-75
Upper Dock branch	72-75
Lydney Tinplate Works	92-96
Middle Forge	6, 108-111
Norchard	112-127
Colliery	112, 115-117, 120-121
Power Station	125-126
Otters Pool Junction, Lydney	56-58
St Mary's Halt	99-100
Severn Bridge station	52-54
Tunnel	55
Severn Railway Bridge	43-51
demolition of	50-51
Sharpness	38-42
Dock	27-37
Oldminster Junction (Sharpness South)	22